How to Draw Manga
For the Beginner
Step By Step Guide to Drawing Manga Characters

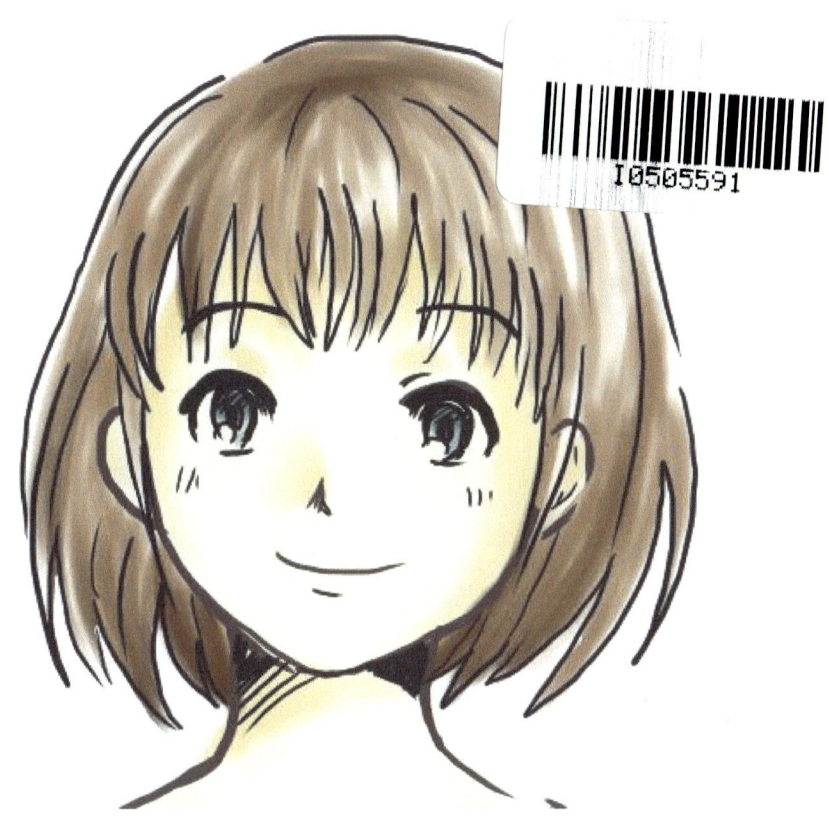

Harriet Kim Anh Rodis
And
John Davidson

Learn to Draw
Book Series
Mendon Cottage Books

JD- Biz Publishing

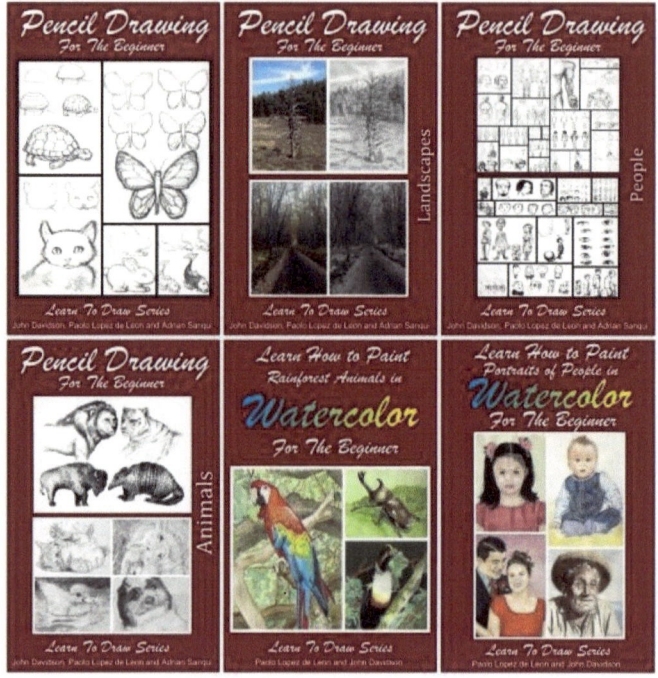

Table of Contents

Introduction

Manga is a kind of comics which originated in Japan. It became popular in all around the world. And if you want to learn the basics of drawing in manga style, this book will provide you the important things you need to know.

Drawing is fun and so is making your own story. You might think that drawing in manga-style is hard and impossible for you to properly do, but with proper technique and style, you can definitely accomplish this.

This is an instructional book meant to help you grasp the basics of manga-style art and to have fun drawing it.

Learn the very basics of drawing easily by following this step-by-step tutorial and realize that drawing is something that is fun to do, and not something that becomes a cause of frustration.

Enjoy drawing!

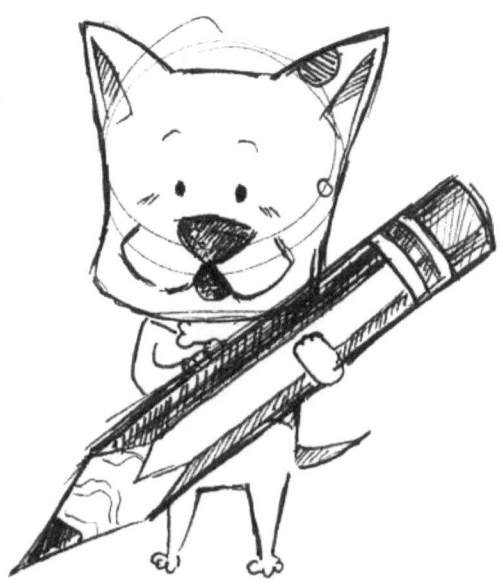

ELEMENTS OF DRAWING

These are the basic and fundamental elements of drawing.

Dot/ Point

•

Lines

Line is defined as series of connecter points that extend from a point to another wherein the edges of the line don't meet.

1) Straight line

Straight lines are lines that don't curve. It can be horizontal, vertical or slanted.

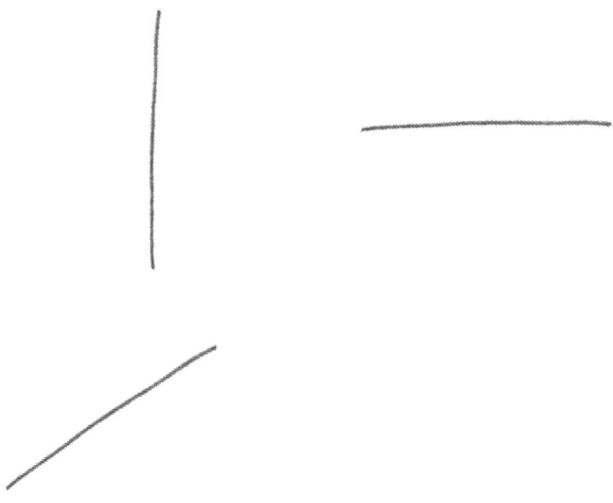

2) Curved line

Curved lines are lines that have curves or gradual change of direction like as shown below.

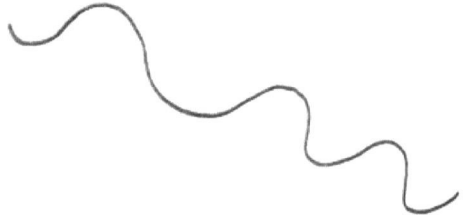

3) **Zigzag line**

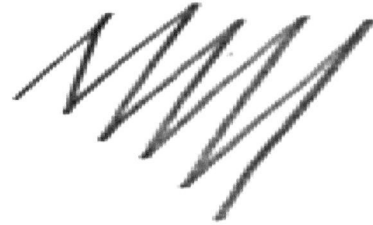

Zigzag lines are lines that form edges as it changes direction.

Shapes
Circle

It is a shape that doesn't have any edges. It can vary in length and width where in it can be oblong.

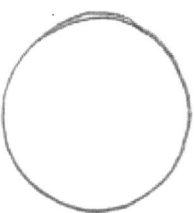

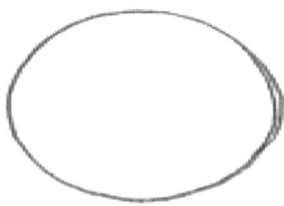

Triangle

It is a shape that has 3 edges.

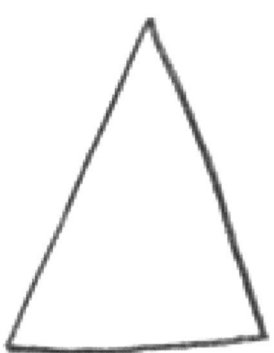

Polygon

These are shapes with "many edges" as its name implies. It includes squares and trapezoids and other shapes with many edges.

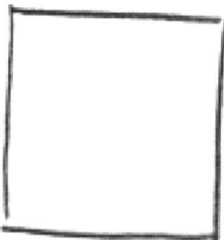

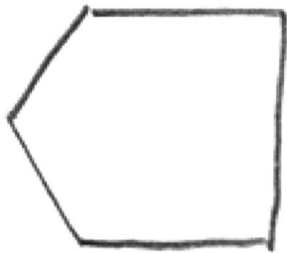

Character

Overview of Character Drawing

Drawing the character from the basics

Everything starts simple and drawing a character, especially if you're a beginner, must start with a draft. And from that point on, you'll add more details.

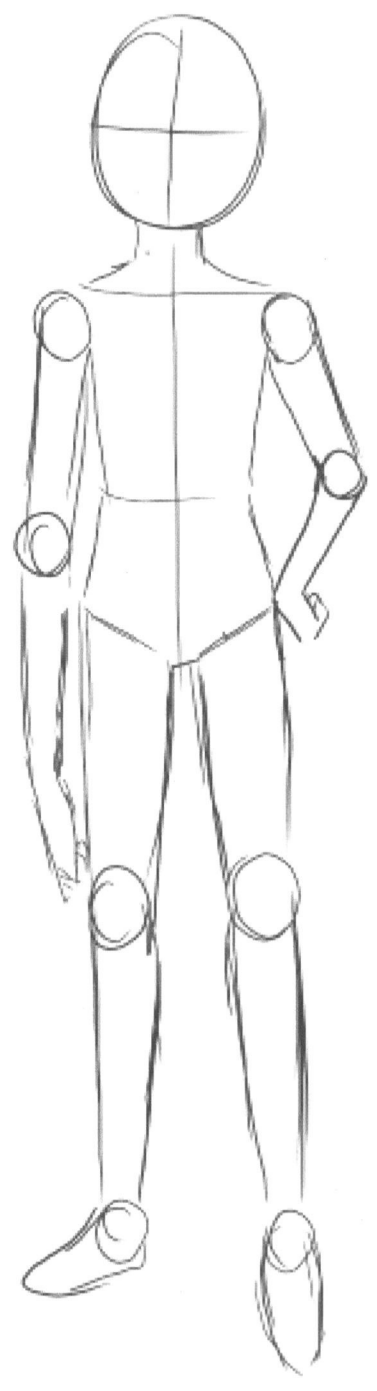

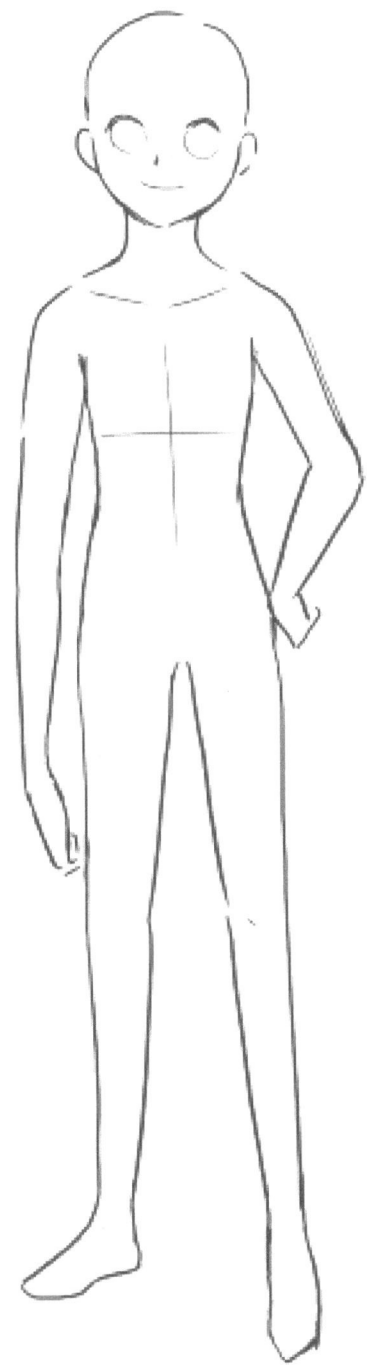

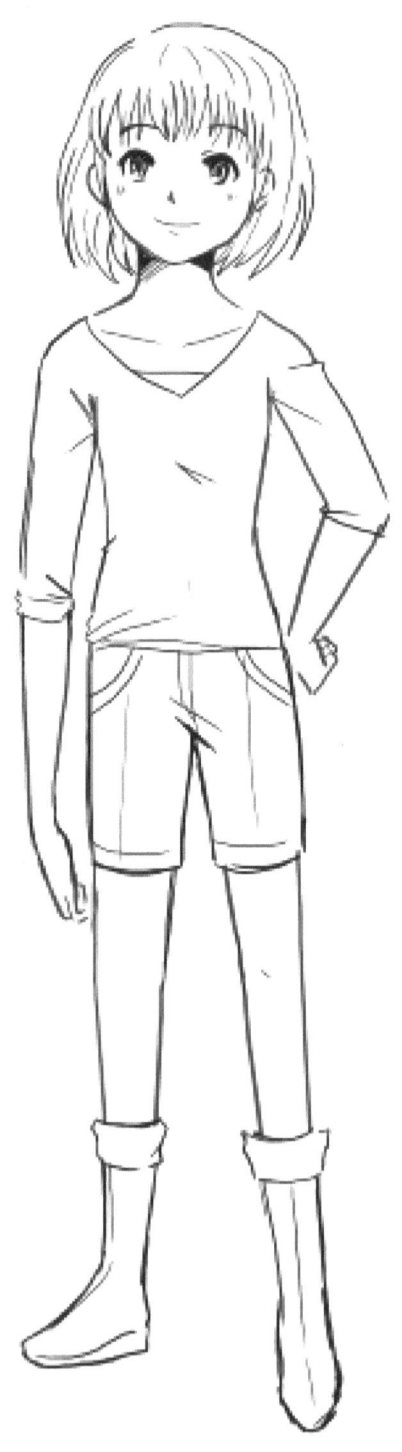

Here is a sample of the "skeleton" draft of the character. You basically use lines and basic shapes for the draft using your pencil. Afterwards still using a pencil, draw the second layer which further shows the body frame of the character. Then, with the pen, draw the basic figure of the character. Add the clothes, the hair, the eyes, etc.

Head

The head is one of the most important parts of a character as it shows the expression. The basic parts of the head that you need to study are the outline of the face, the hair, the eyes, the ears, the mouth and the nose. After that, let's go to the expression which can be showed using the combination of the mouth and the eyes.

OUTLINE OF THE FACE

Start with an oblong. Then add the lines where you want the eyes and the other part of the face to be. This will act as guideline where you should place them. The vertical line in the face shows where the head is facing. It acts as the center line where you should align the nose and the mouth sooner.

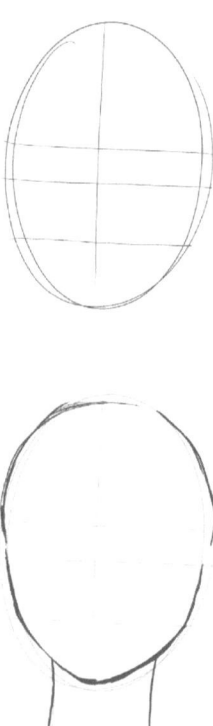

Then add the jaw line and the top part of the head. It actually depends on your style of drawing. You can use pointed jaws or nicely curved jaw lines. Just be sure that the left and right parts of the face are symmetrical.

One way of drawing an outline of the face is the use of circle then after that, adding the jaw line. This is certainly helpful in drawing the side view though you can also use the first technique.

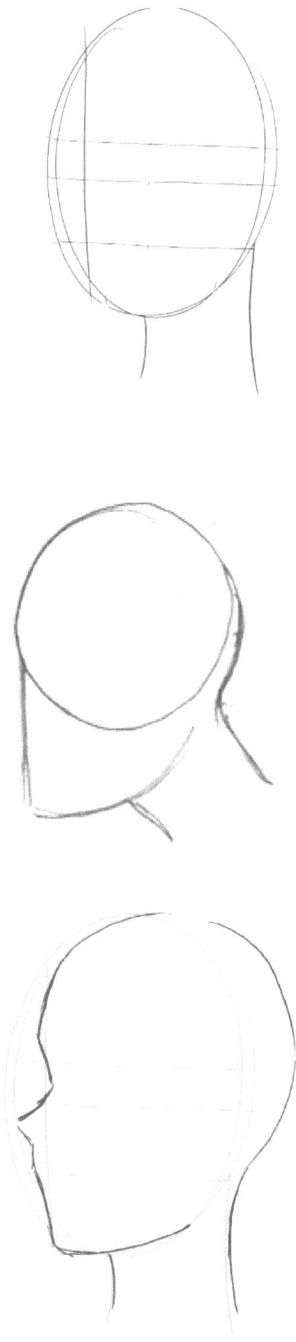

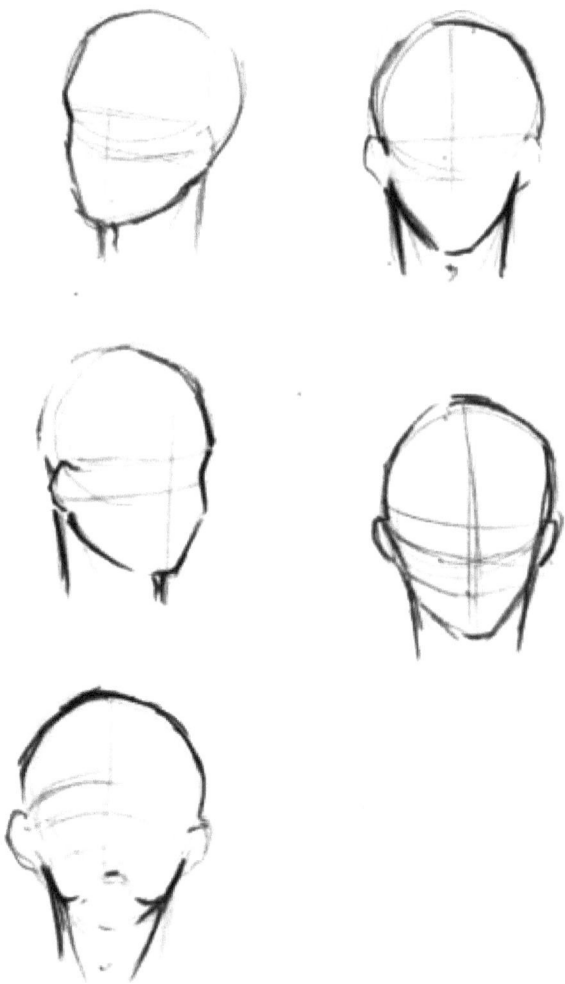

The face outline can also vary in different ways depending on the direction the head is facing.

What is shown on the right side is some of the head varieties depending on the direction it is facing. The lines can vary every direction. For example, when the head is facing up, the lines are curved up and when the head is facing down, the lines are curved downward.

It is shown below how to make the head depending on where is facing. Here it started with an oblong, then the central line is added. This central line determines where it is facing.

The other lateral lines are added and adjusted to where the eyes, nose and mouth should be placed.

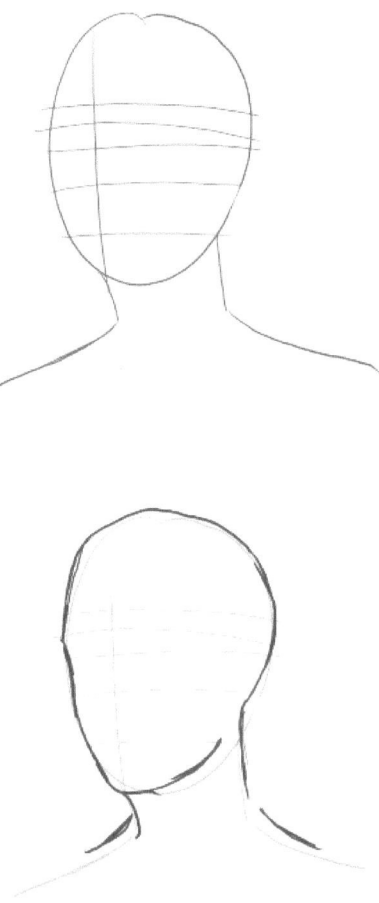

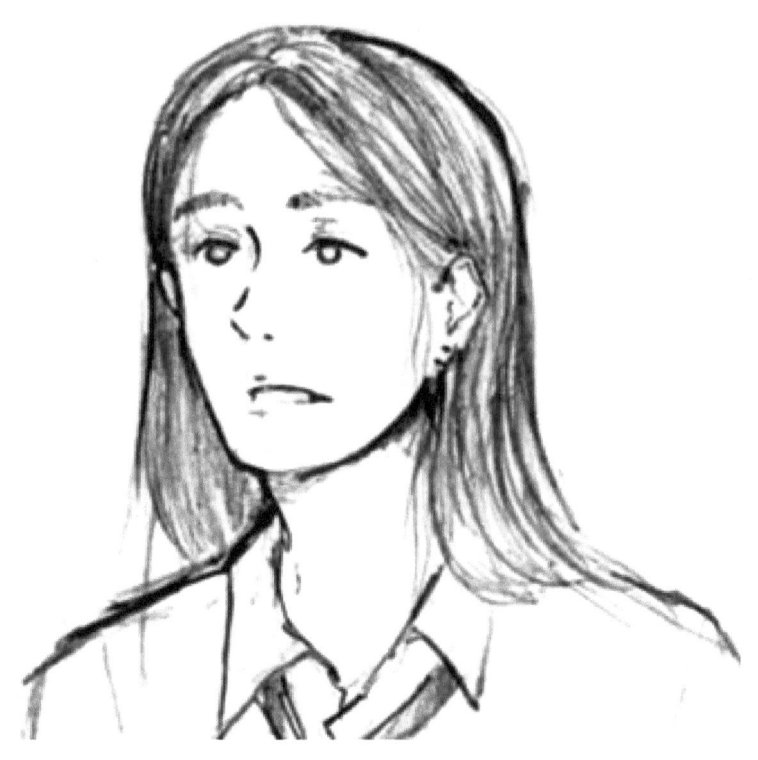

EYES

Next to be discussed is the eyes. The eyes is the main ingredient for expression. There are different techniques on how to make the eyes. This depends on your drawing style. But here, we'll discuss and show 2 different techniques mostly used.

Using V as Guideline

Using a pencil, draw lightly a "V" wherein the length is equal to the length you want the eyes to be. Use the "V" as guideline to the upper and lower part of the eyes and also the eyebrows. After that, add the other details such as the iris of the eyes and the shading of the eyes. Erase the pencil.

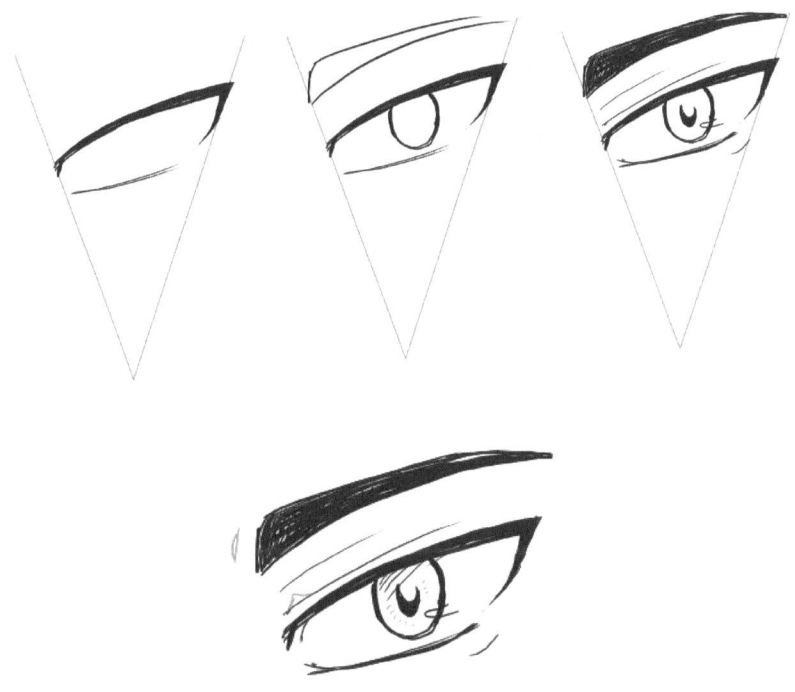

Example 1.

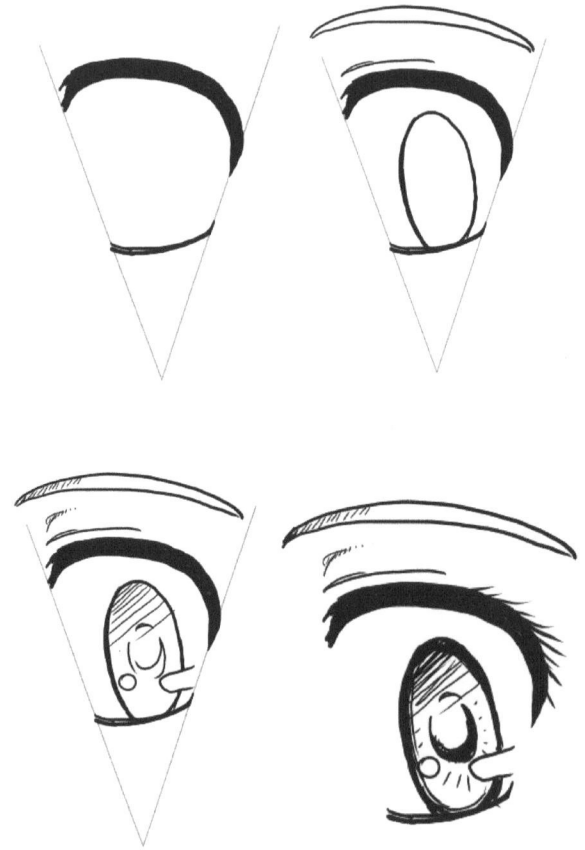

Example 2.

Using Circle/Oblong as Guideline

First, lightly draw a circle using a pencil. The circle can be imperfect. You can even use an oblong for thinner eyes.

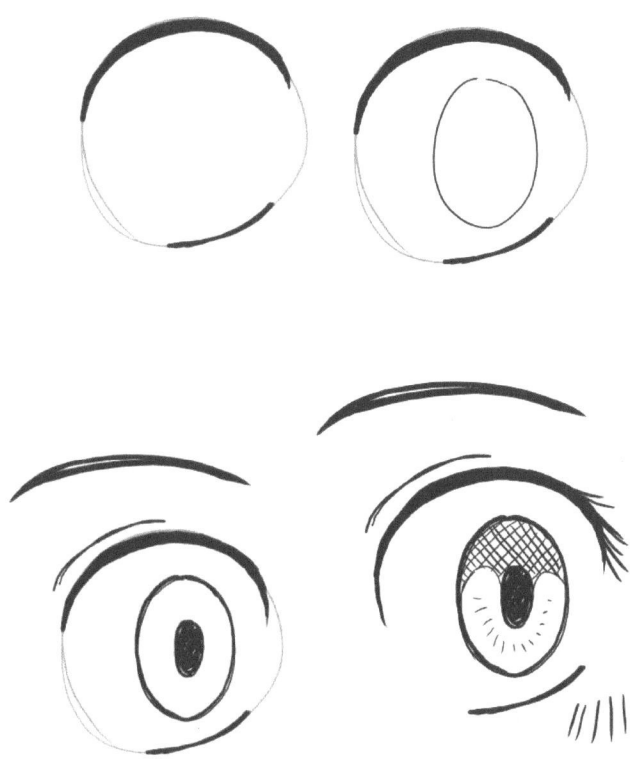

Example 1.

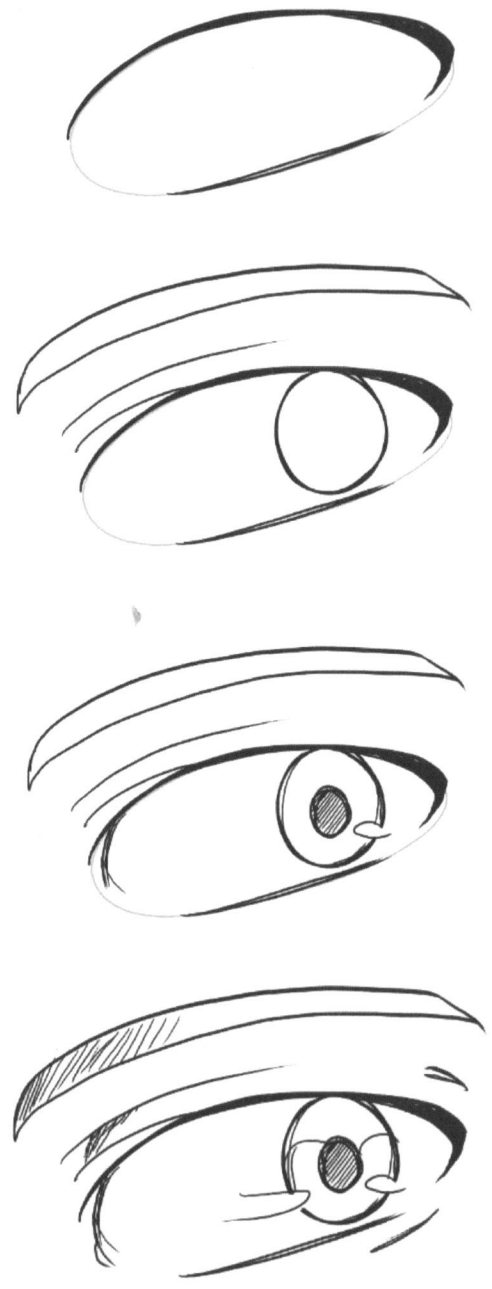

Example 2.

NOSE

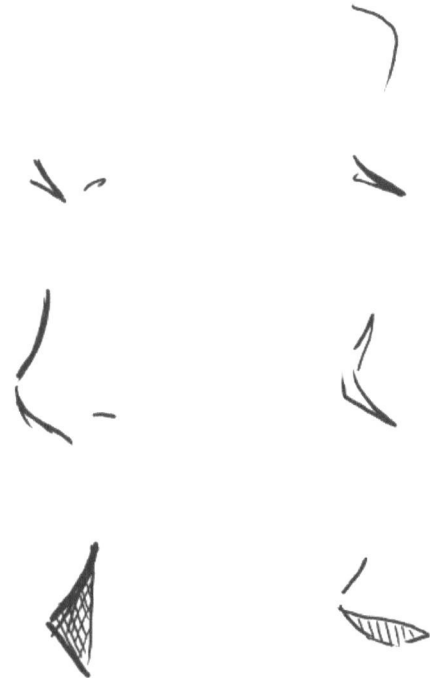

The nose is a part of the face that is important though it may not look like it.

On the right side are some drawings of nose. Again, it totally depends on your drawing style. You can experiment on the nose how often you want.

Where to place the nose?

The guidelines you made will determine that. It is most preferred that you put the nose a level lower than the eyes as shown in the drawing below.

In the side views, you can also experiment with the nose but you should also follow the guidelines that you made and make sure that the side view version of the nose matches with the front version. You don't want a character that changes nose when it faces a different direction.

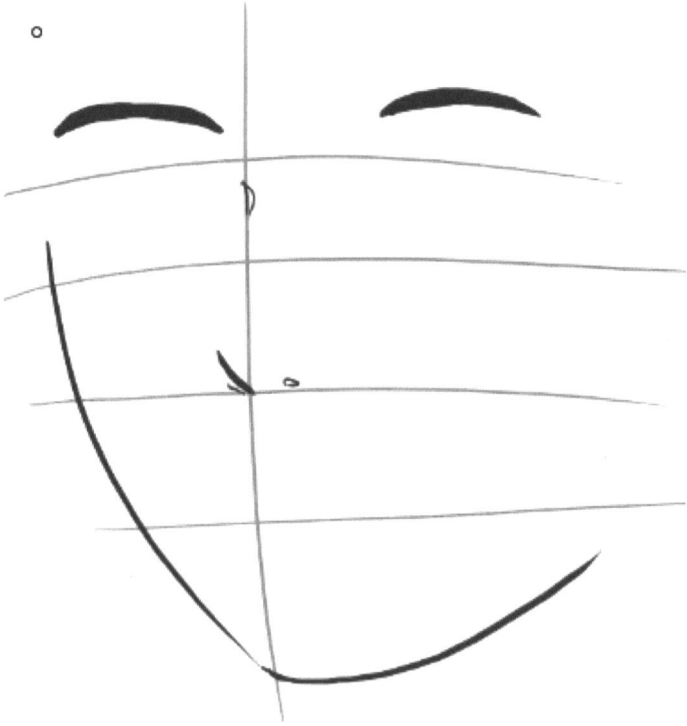

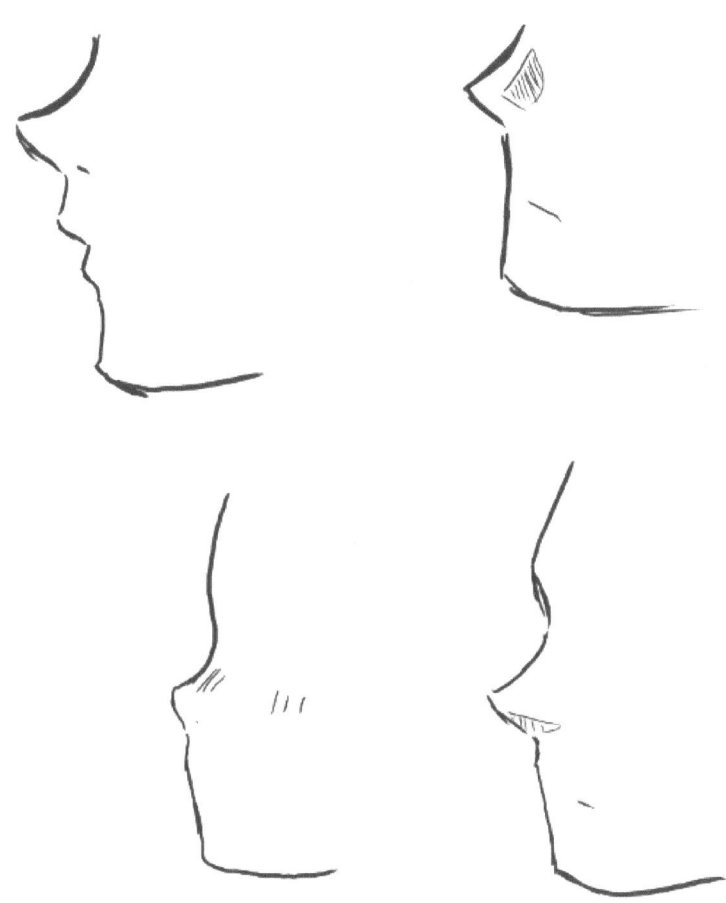

MOUTH

The mouth has a lot of effect in the total expression of the character. It can show happiness, sadness, excitement, anger and other kind of expressions.

Below are some examples of mouths showing different kinds of expressions.

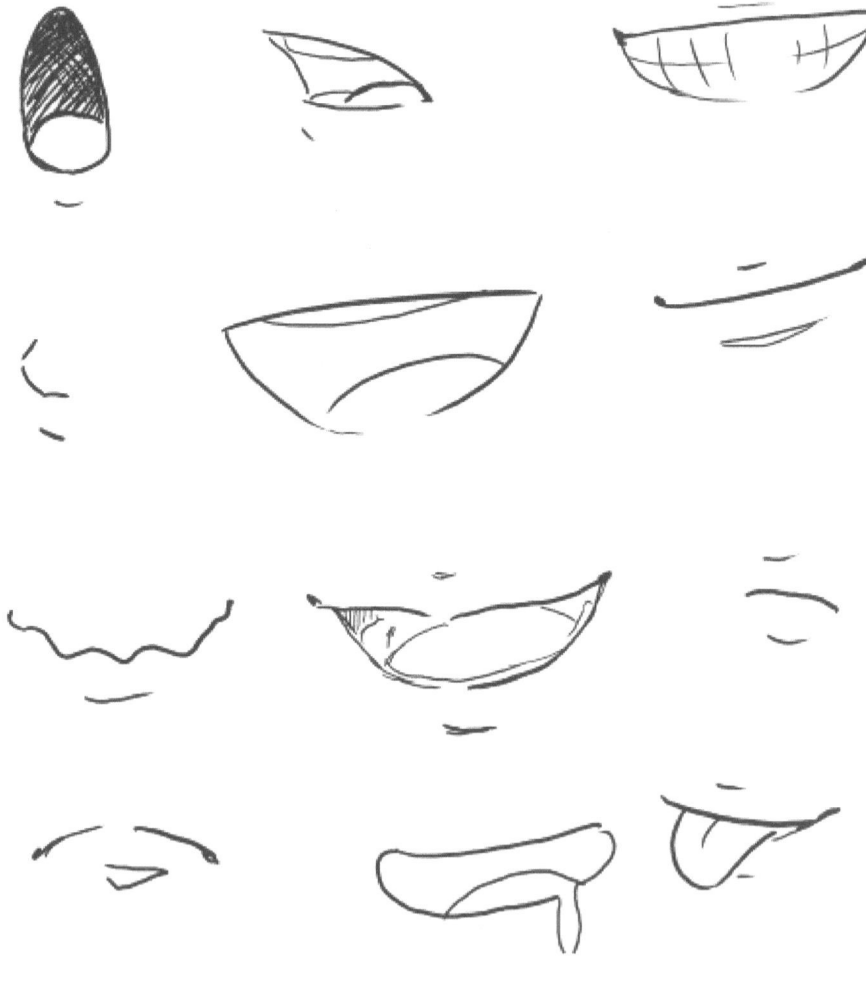

EARS

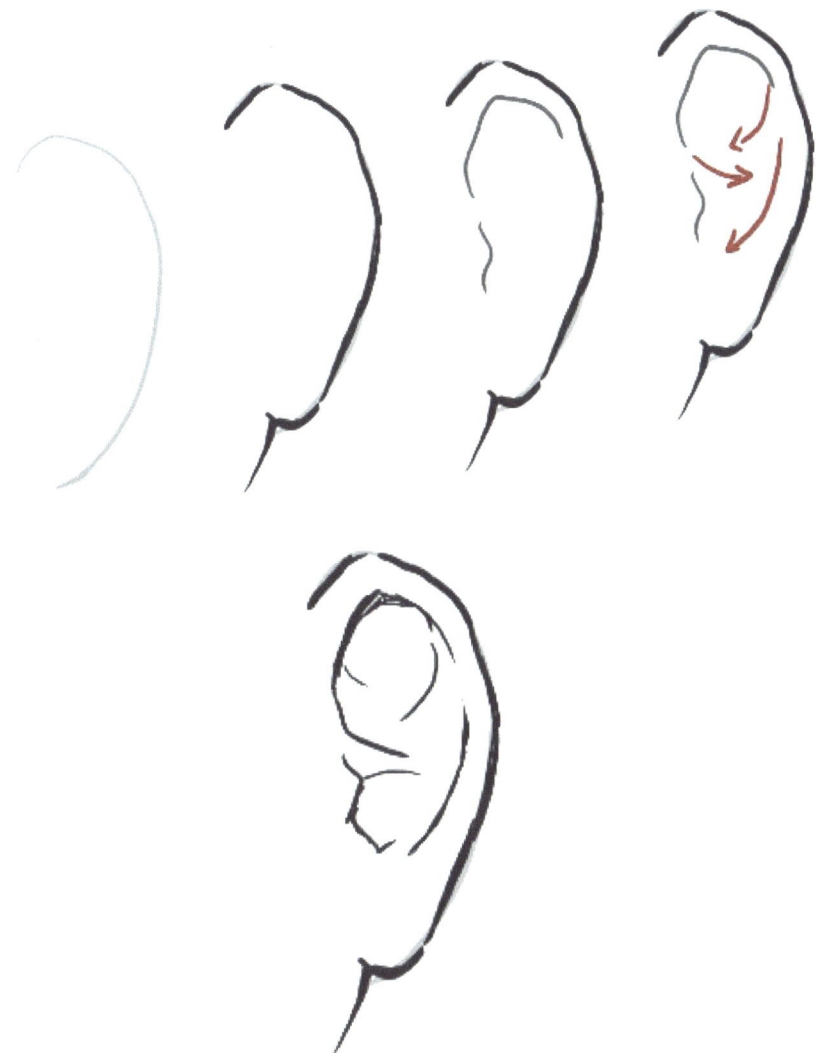

To beginners, ears are drawn as half circle near the eyes but to improve on drawing the ears, that's where you will start.

As shown below, a semi-circle is lightly drawn using a pencil. Then the outline of the ears is drawn next. You can follow and copy how the ears is drawn below. But when you get the principle of drawing the ears, you can experiment on your style and apply it on your character.

Here it is shown the basic creases in the ears as shown by the red arrows.

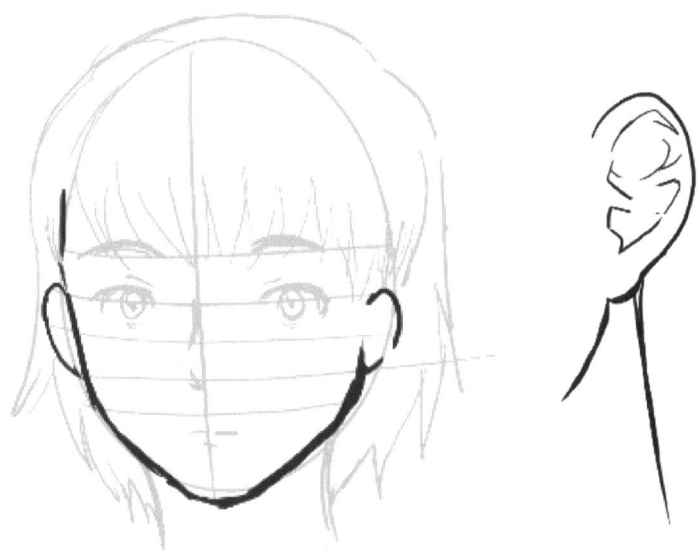

Where to draw the ears then? In the guidelines of the head which we have shown, there is a line that runs through the half of the face. Then there's also a line that runs through where you'll put the nose. Between those 2 lines, that's what you'll use as guideline to where you'll put the ears.

Coloring

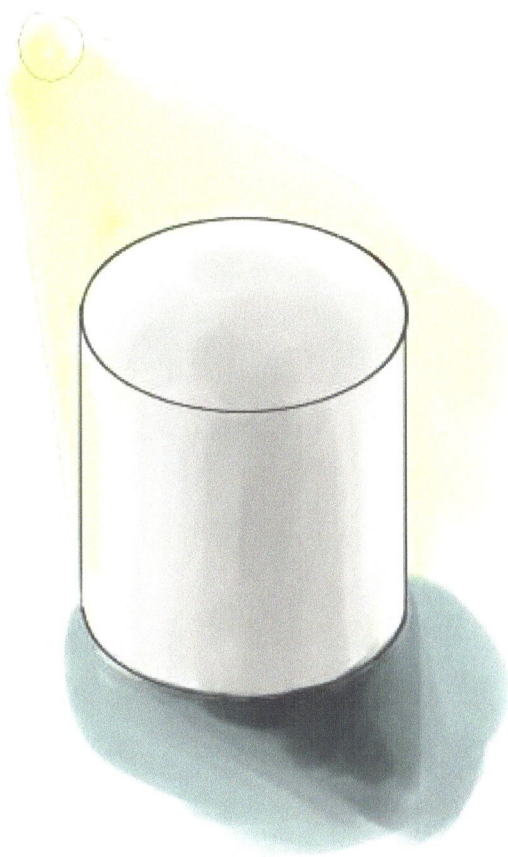

When coloring the character, you should also consider the shadows and light.

An example is shown on the left side. The shadow is placed in the opposite of the light source. The back of the cylinder has darker color than what is in front of the light source. It also casts a shadow on the ground.

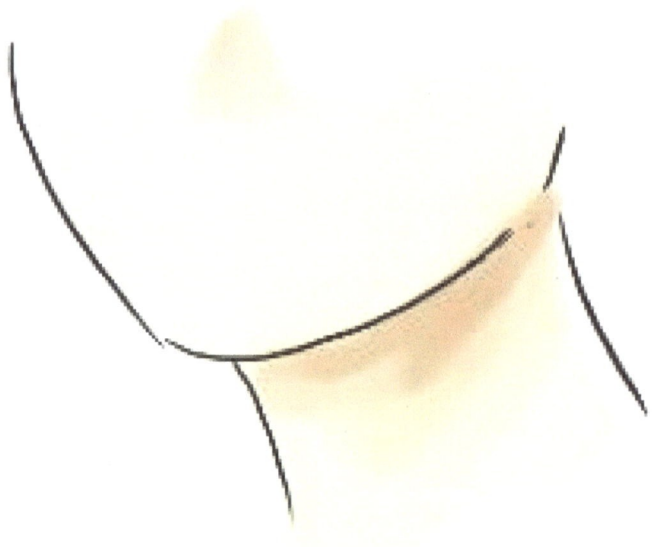

Same principle is applied throughout the coloring stage. You should take note of the light and shadows. In coloring the neck for example, you'll add darker and more powerful color below the jaws. This adds more effect showing the texture and the shape of the object.

COLORING THE CHARACTER

When you're coloring your manga character, it is preferred to start with the skin color. Next is the hair then the clothes.

To show you the step by step coloring of the character, we'll use the character which we made from the start of the book.

Skin

When coloring the skin, the first tone is added. This is called the base color of the skin. Afterwards, you should add the second layer which is the second tone. This is put where the shadow shows up in the skin like on the neck, knees, legs and underneath the bangs and hair. The second tone could be darker and more powerful than the base color.

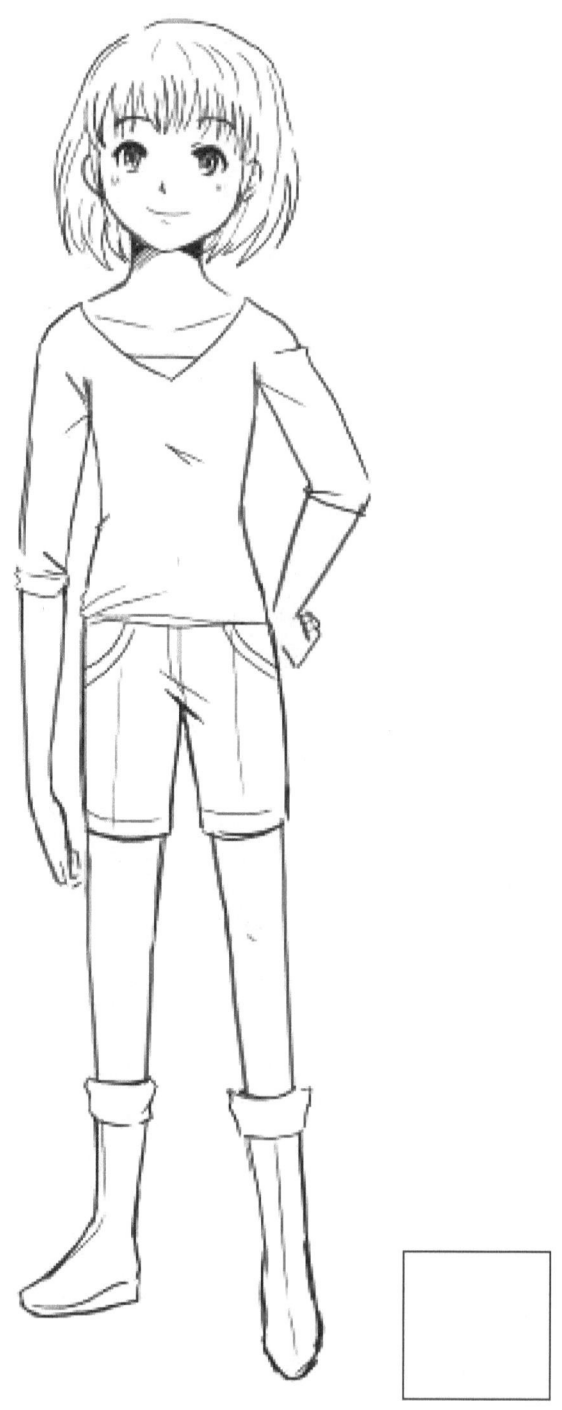

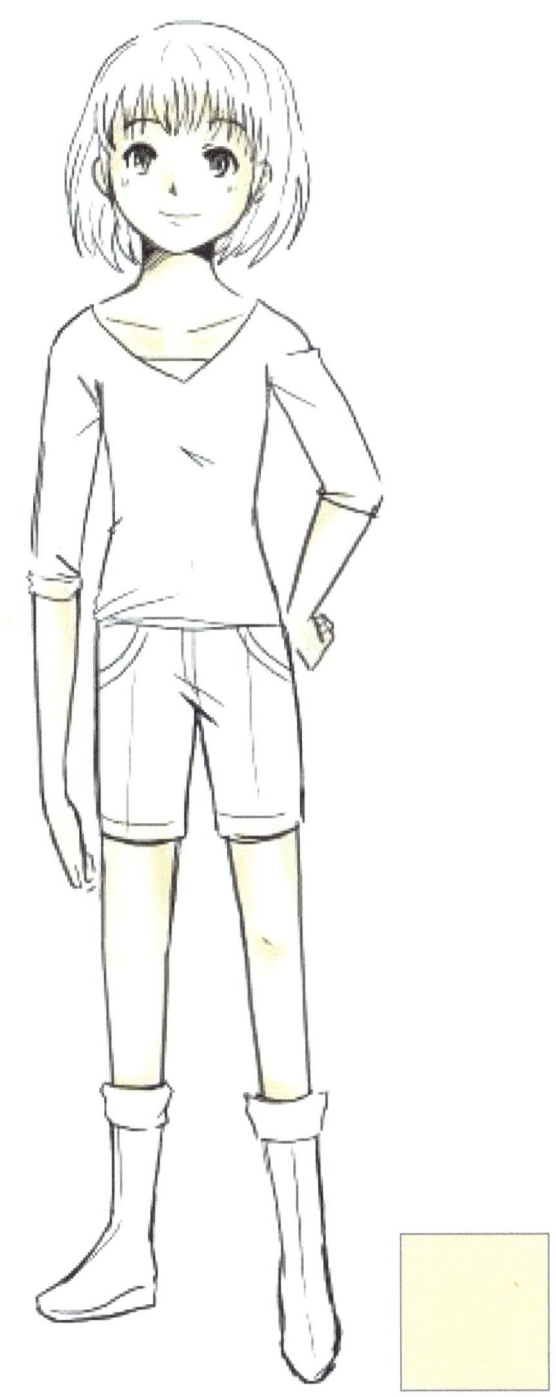

Hair

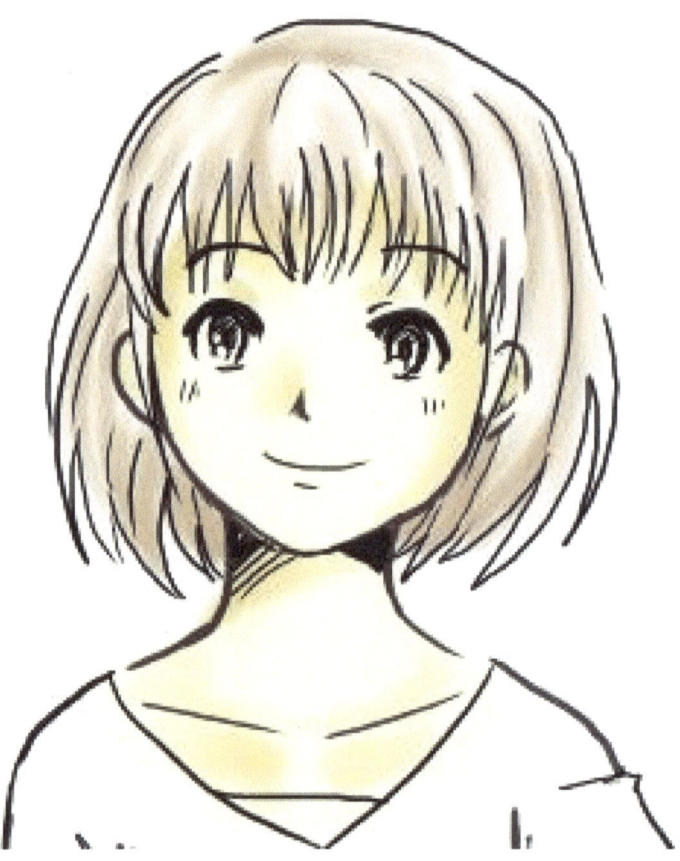

Same principle applies with coloring the hair. Apply the base color then add the shadowing. It can take to multiple layers.

As shown in the left side, the base colors are added. Here the artist used a very light brown a little darker is added in the parts that should be shown darker. This will make the hair come alive.

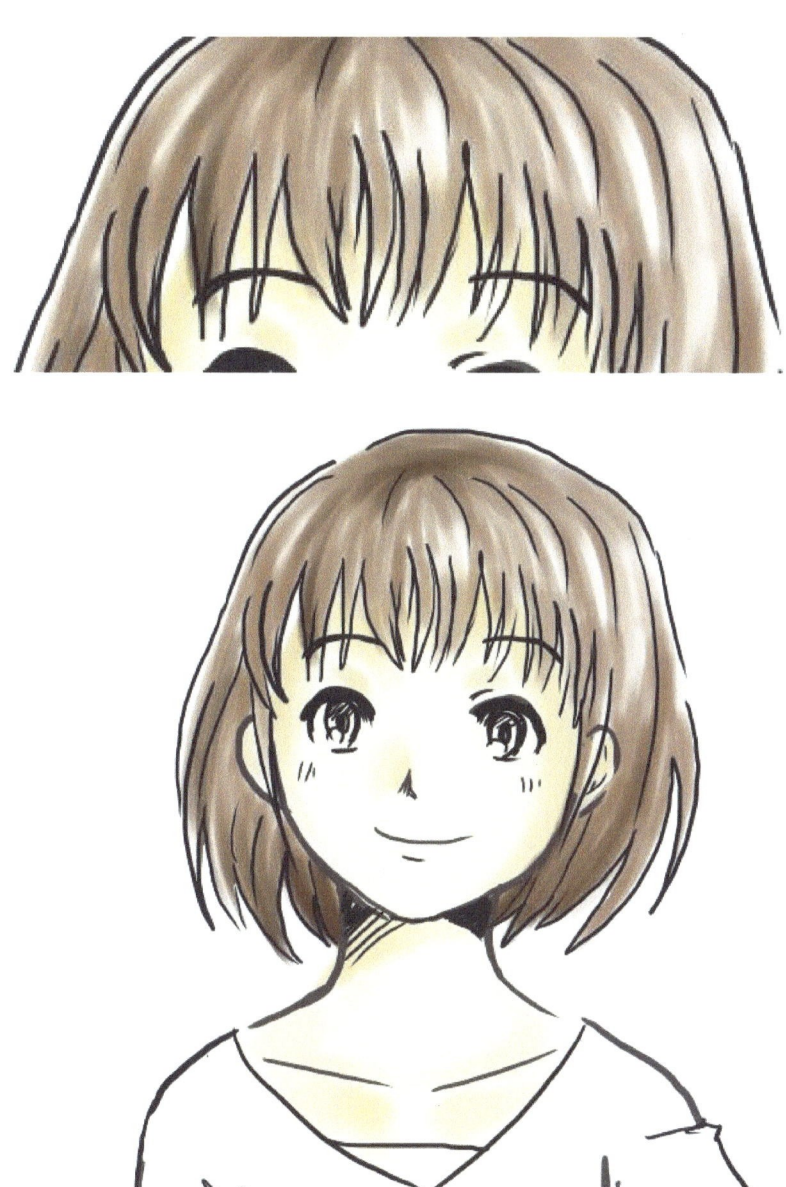

Afterwards, a much darker brown is applied. You can see here that where the light hits the hair, the darker brown is not applied. This will, again, bring more life to the hair.

Eyes

The eyes is one of the parts of the face that catches more attention. It reflects the character—it's personality. You can experiment in coloring the eyes of the

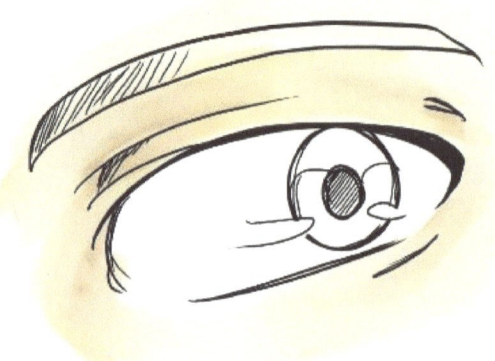

Here is a step by step procedure of coloring the eyes after coloring the skin. You can use a mixture of mediums in doing this like watercolor and color pencil, or way better, specialized marker pens.

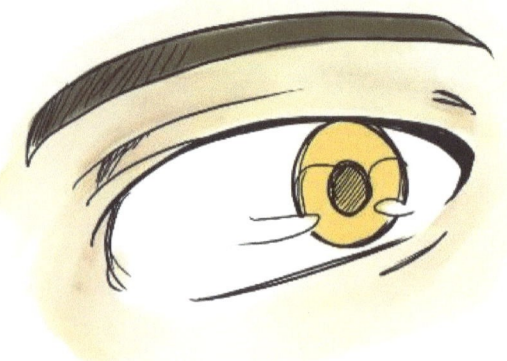

Next is adding the base color of the eyes and the eye brows. Here the artist used an orange color as the base color.

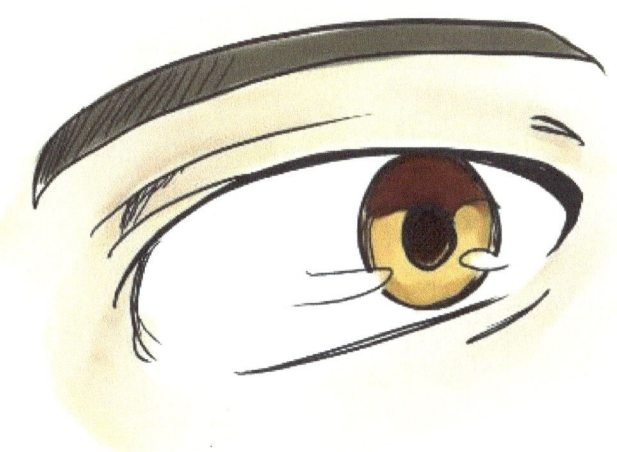

Then darker color is added in the top part of the eyes. This is the second layer of coloring. Some hints of the same color is also added in the margin of the iris.

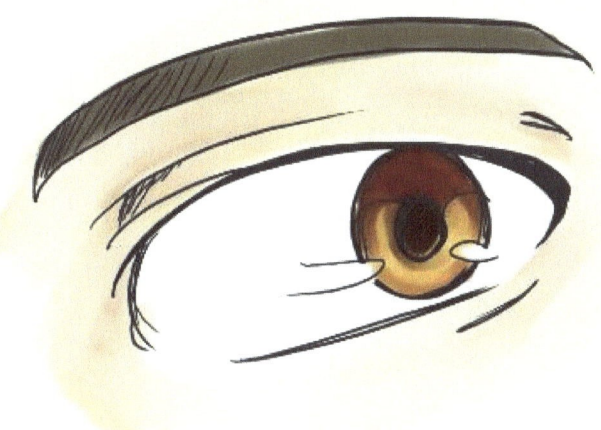

If you're using a watercolor, blend the second tone in the margin of the iris avoiding the lighter portion like as shown.

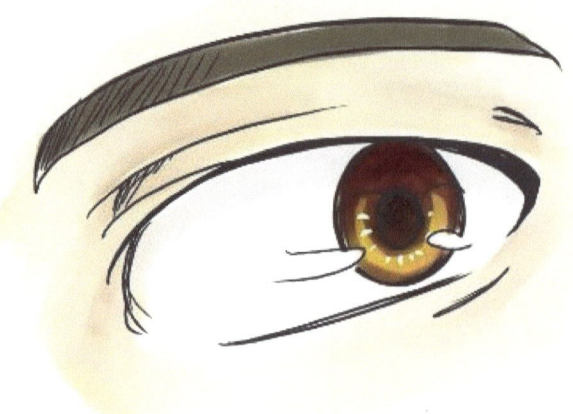

Then, add a brighter color on the lighter portion to create a powerful impression. Then you can add more details according to your style. Here, the artist also added white bands along the eyes.

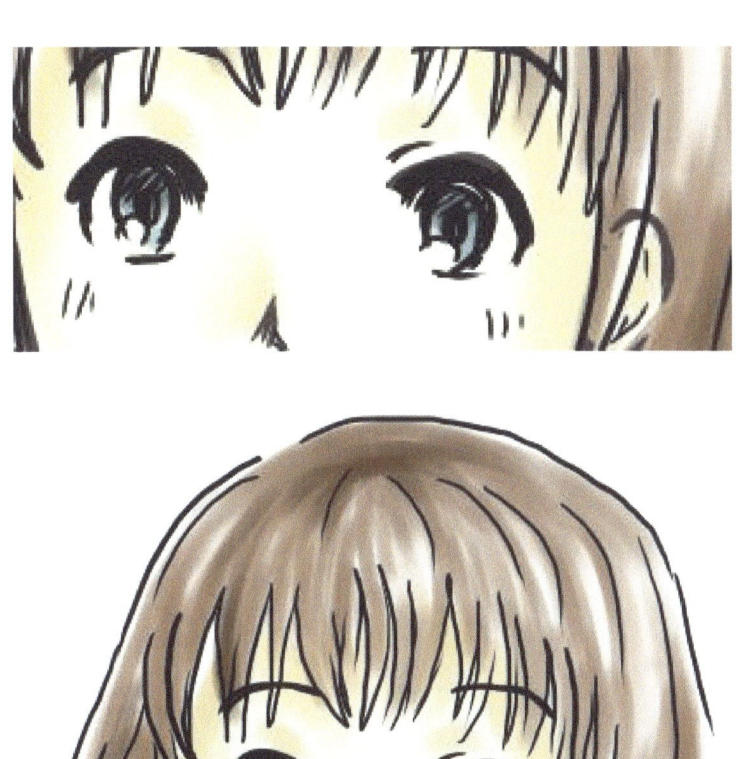

Same principle was applied with the sample character.

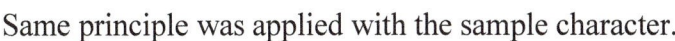

Clothes

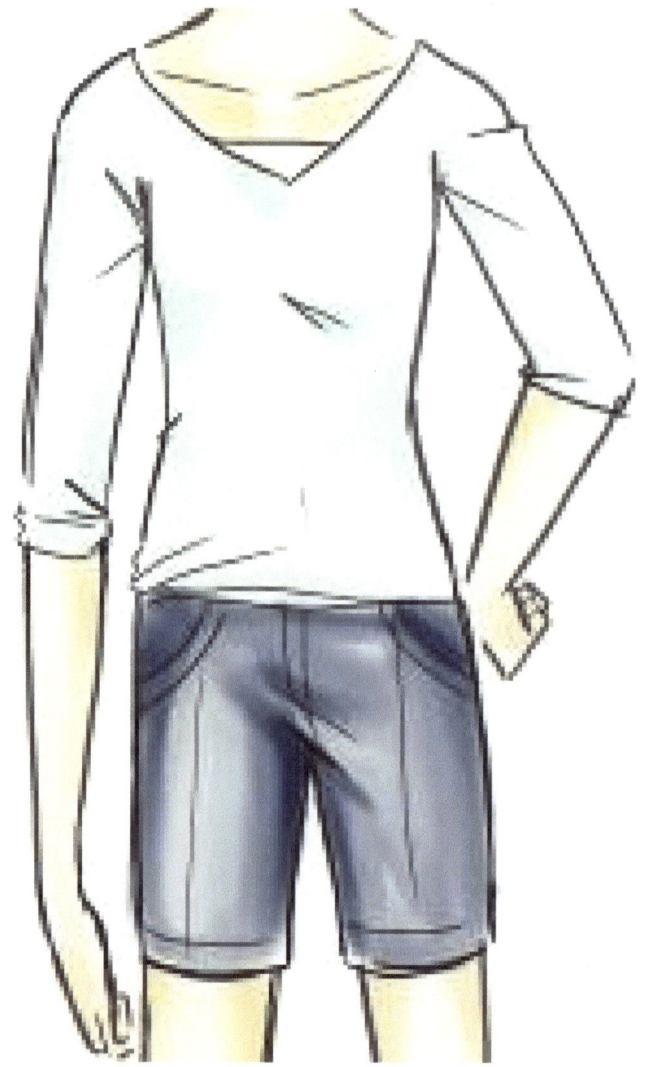

In doing the clothes, you basically color the dark parts of the clothes—the creases and the folds.

Using the same principle in coloring, you start with the base color. For example in the pants, we used a light blue color then soon added a darker navy blue color to depict the shadows.

In the shoes, the artist used the same principle by using a grey color then adding a dark brown for the shadows.

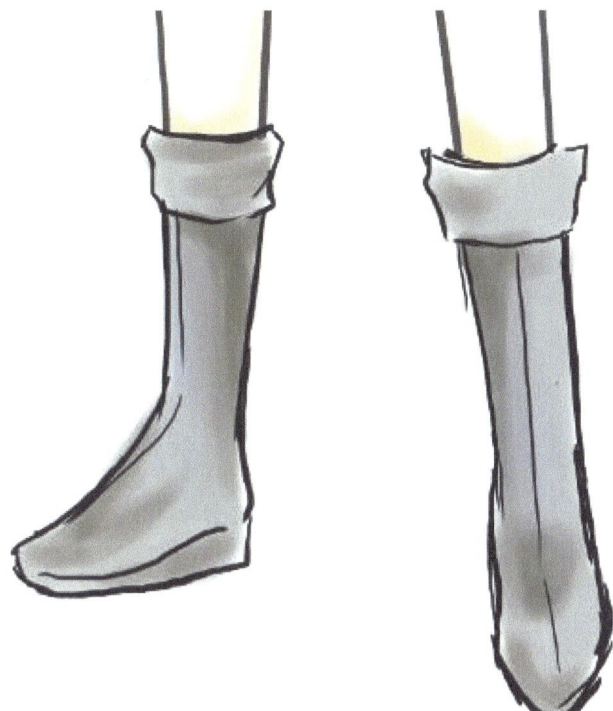

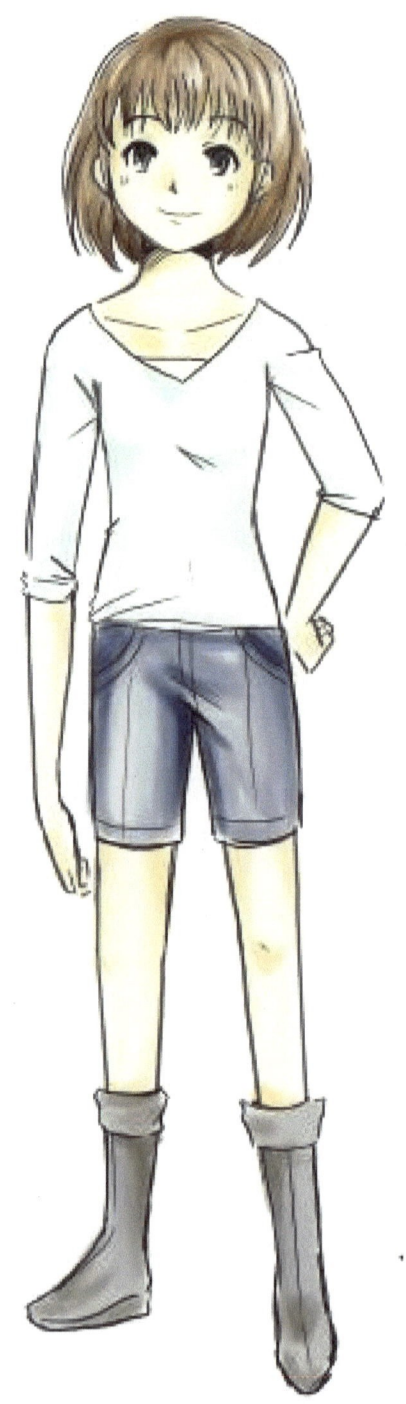

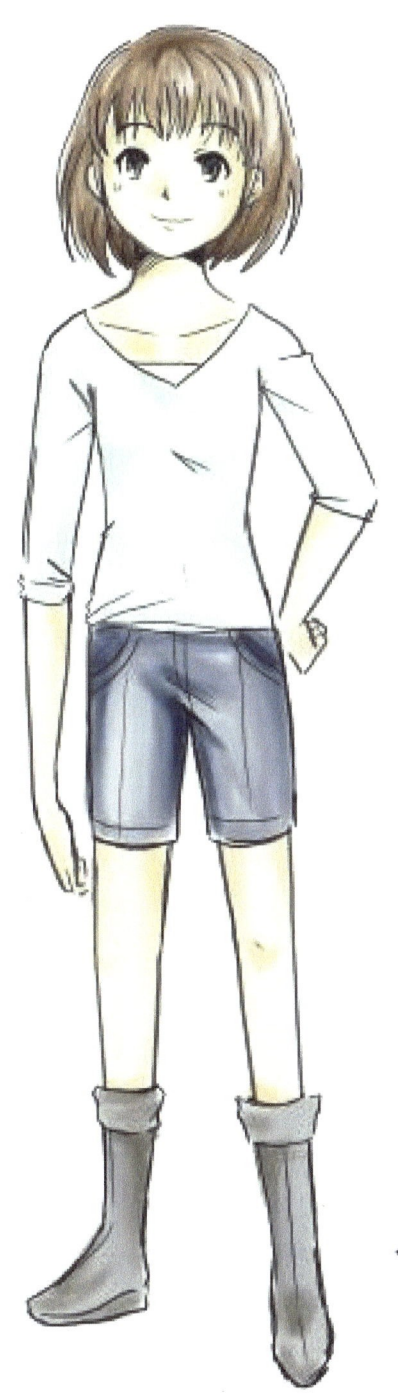

Viola! Our character is done!

Example 2

Another example is shown below. Starting from the draft of the body, the main outline of the character is made.

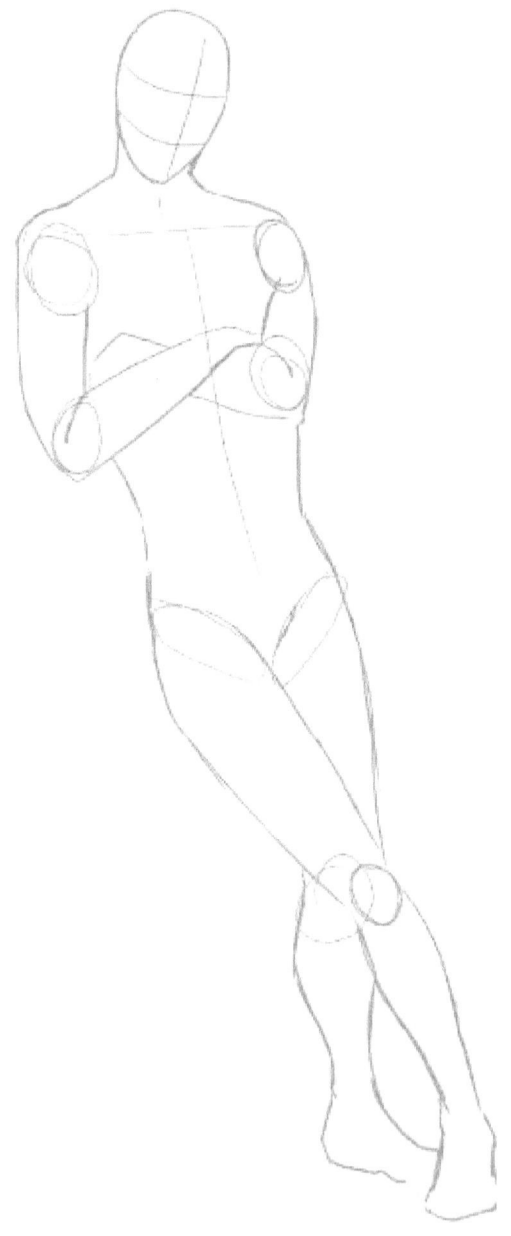

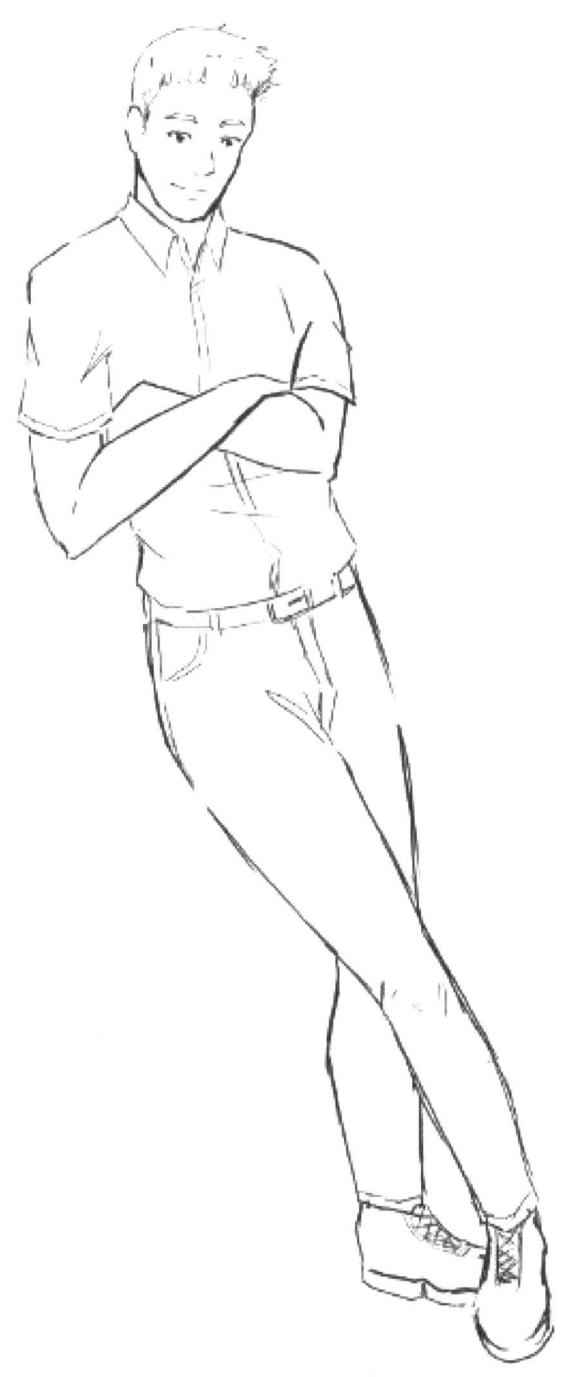

The first thing to do in coloring it is to start with the base color.

The first thing to do in coloring it is to start with the base color. Then the artist added the orange-brown shadows of the skin. Then add the color of the hair. Same principle was used. The base color was added first then the second layer of dark brown.

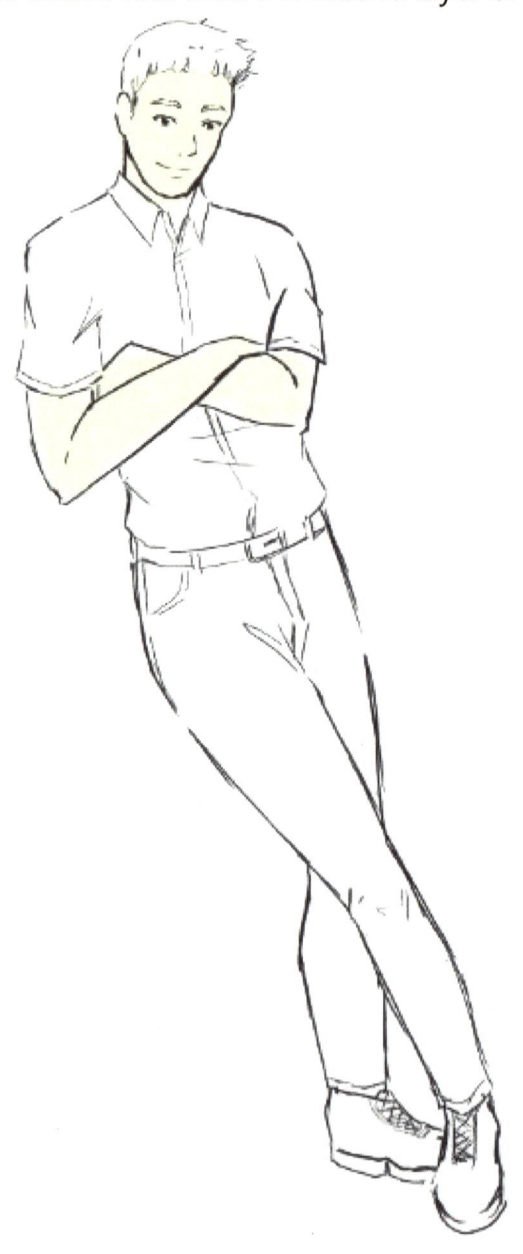

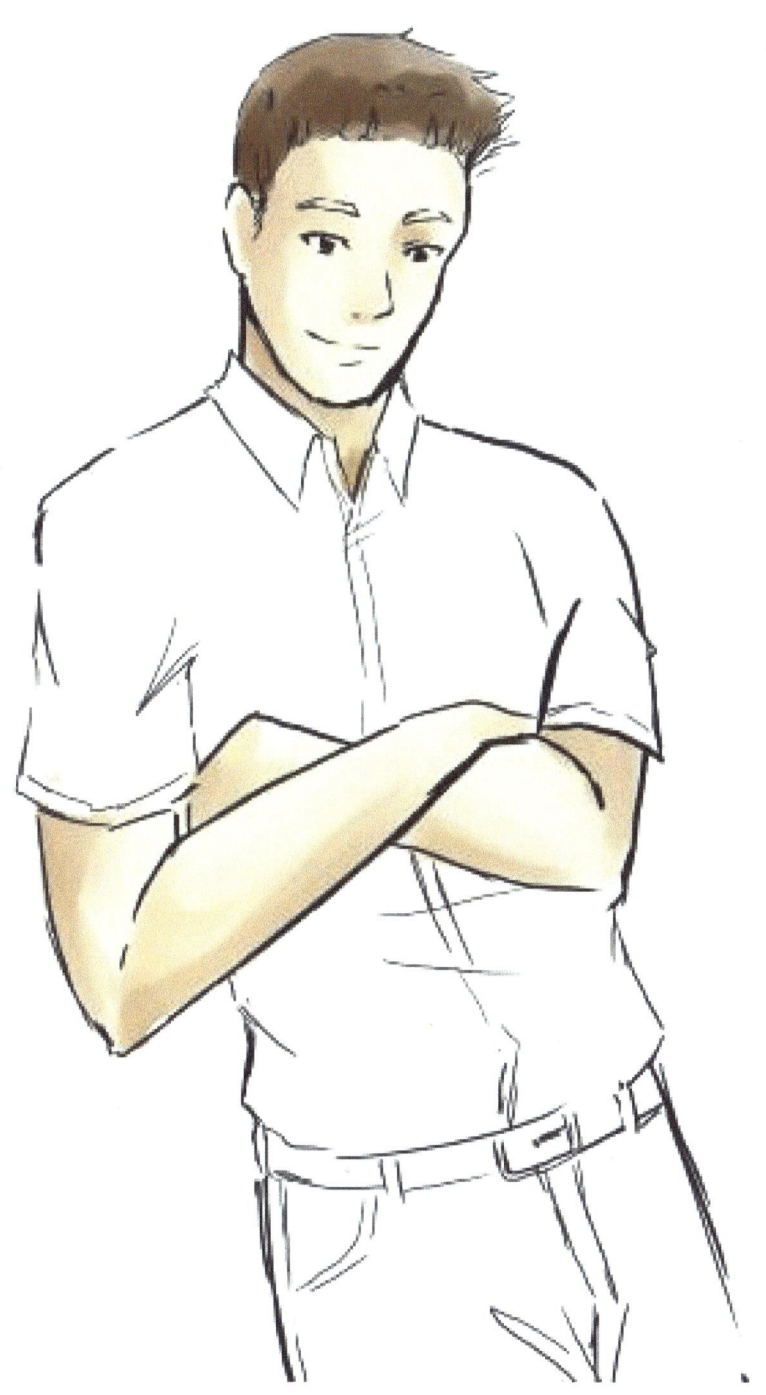

Same principle with the clothes. But here you will see that where the light is, it is avoided to be colored. Then after that. The second layer of color was added to the places there should be shadows.

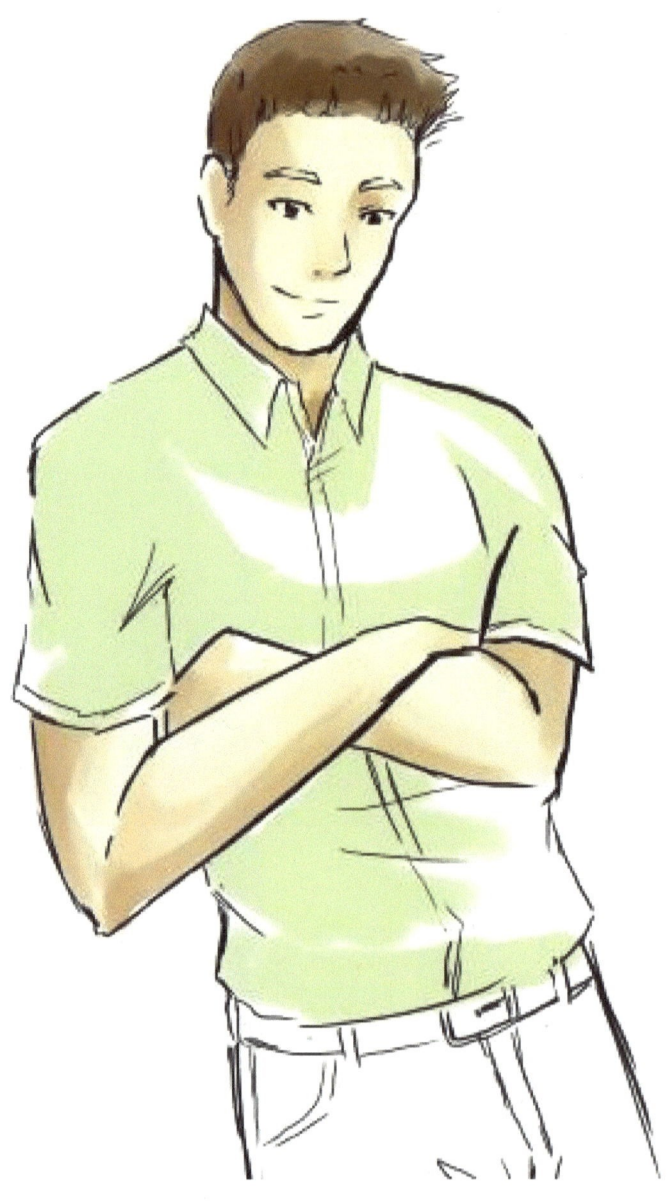

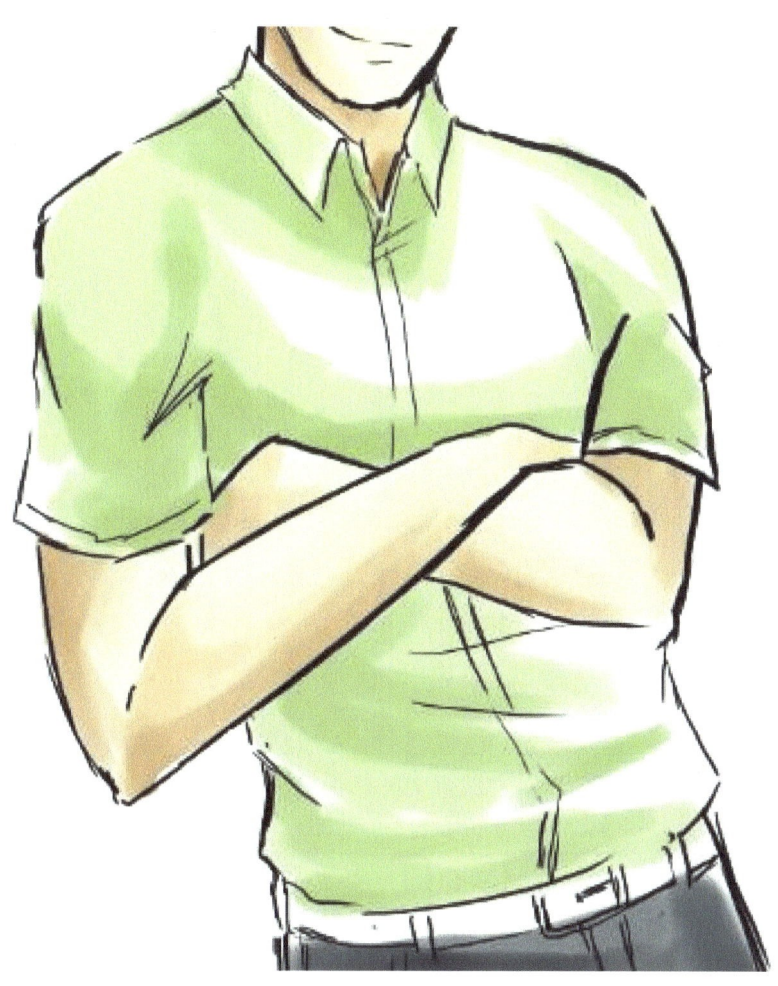

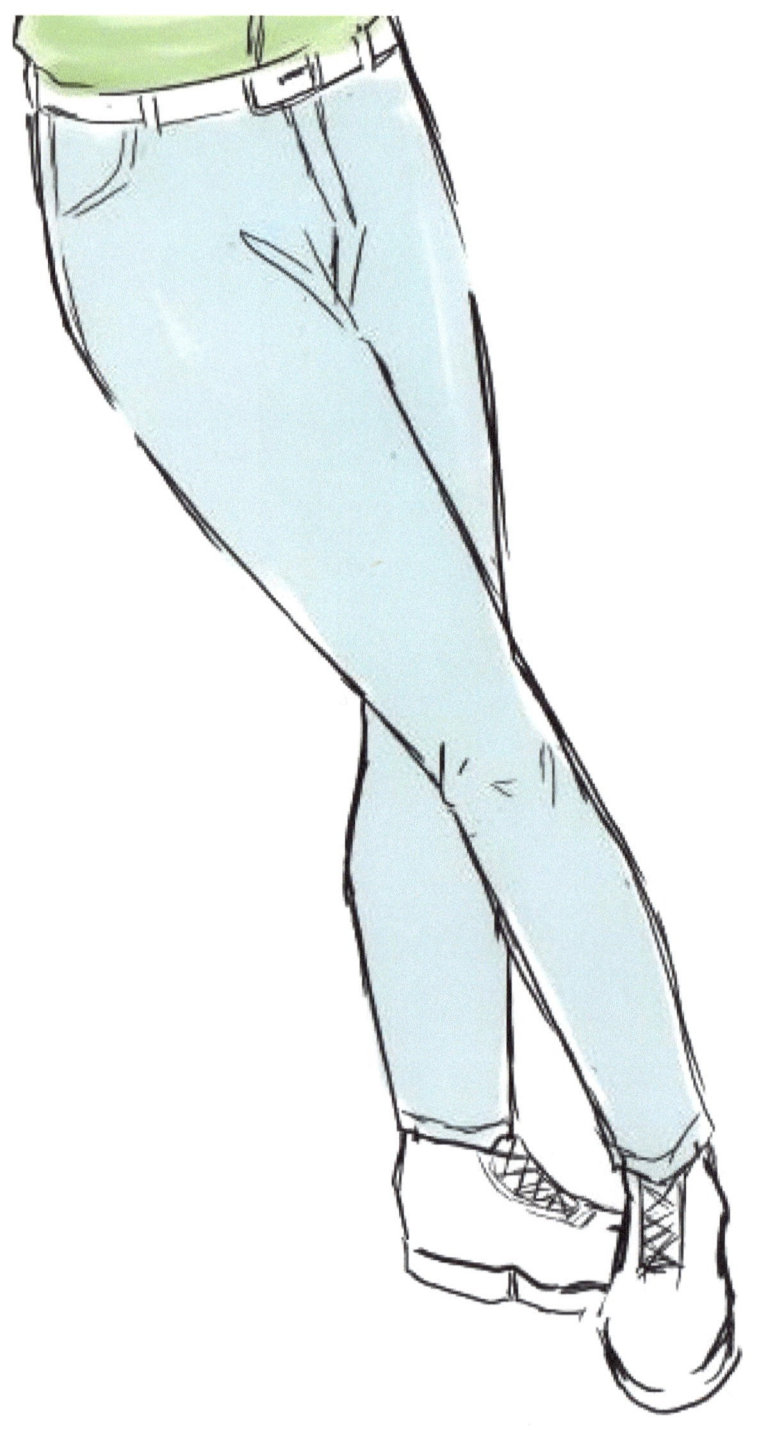

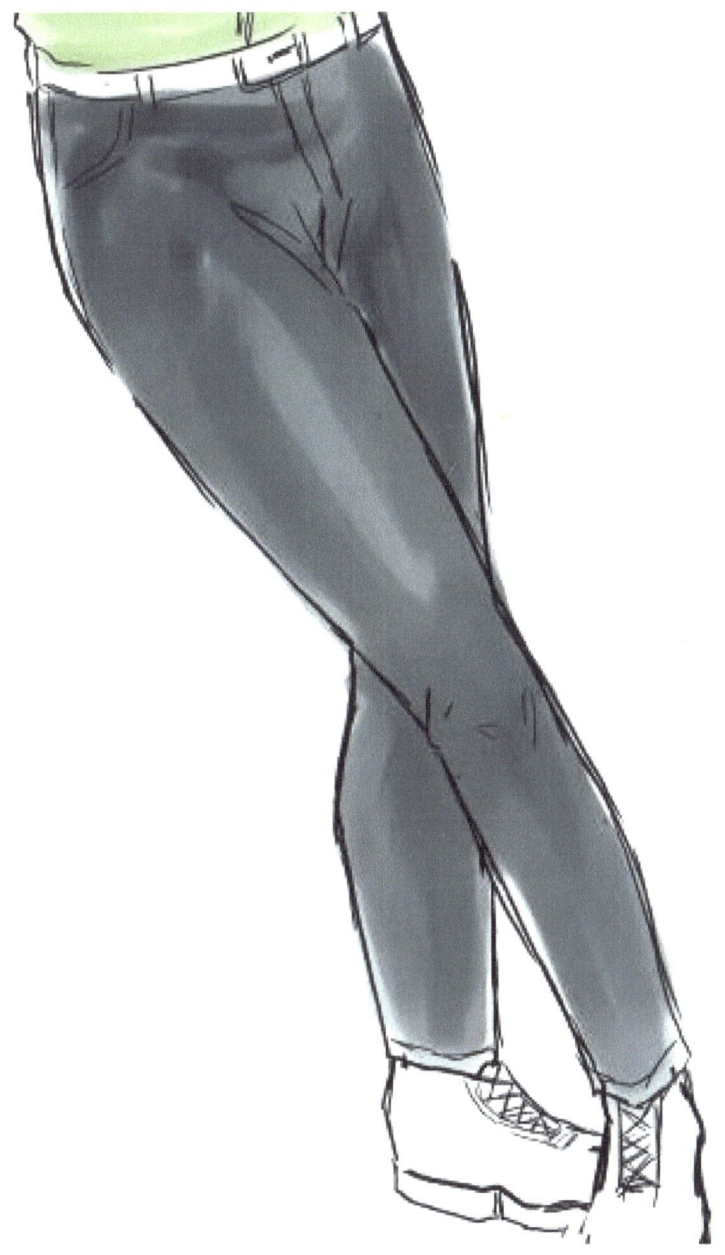

In the pants, a light blue color was added as the first tone. Then a darker navy blue to the pants which will give it a feeling that the one that the character is wearing is pants. Also, it is done with avoiding the light part of the pants.

The shoes can be done using the same principle.

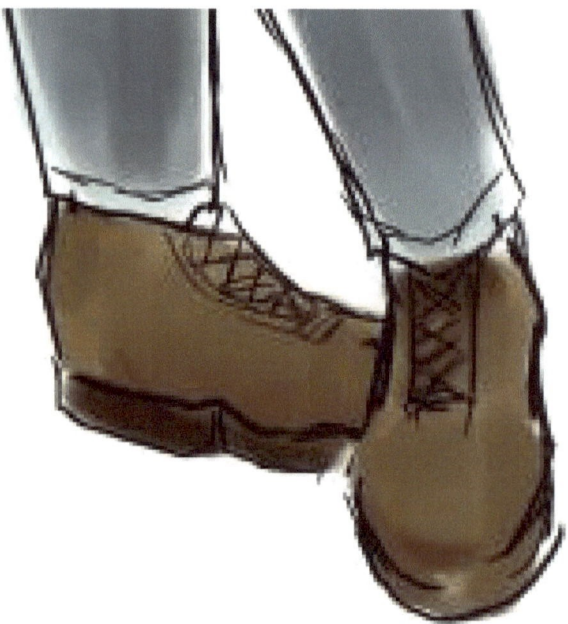

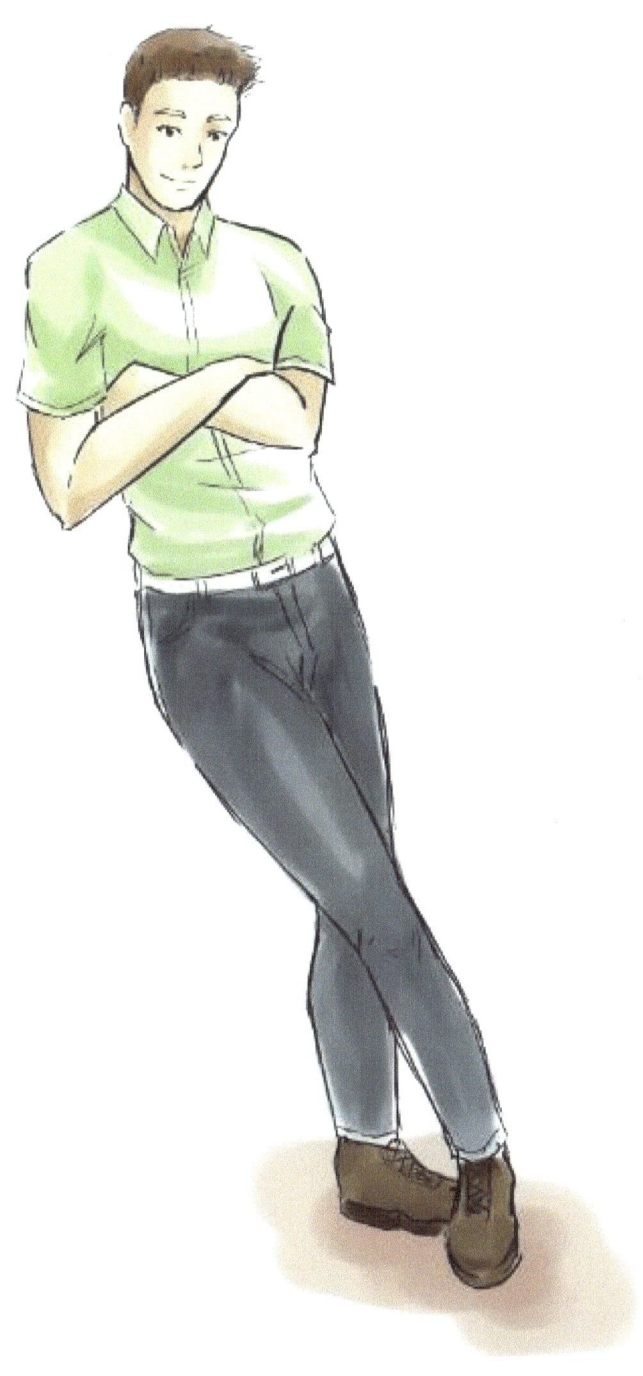

Done!

Example 3
Starting with the black and white line drawing, we begin with
the skin color.

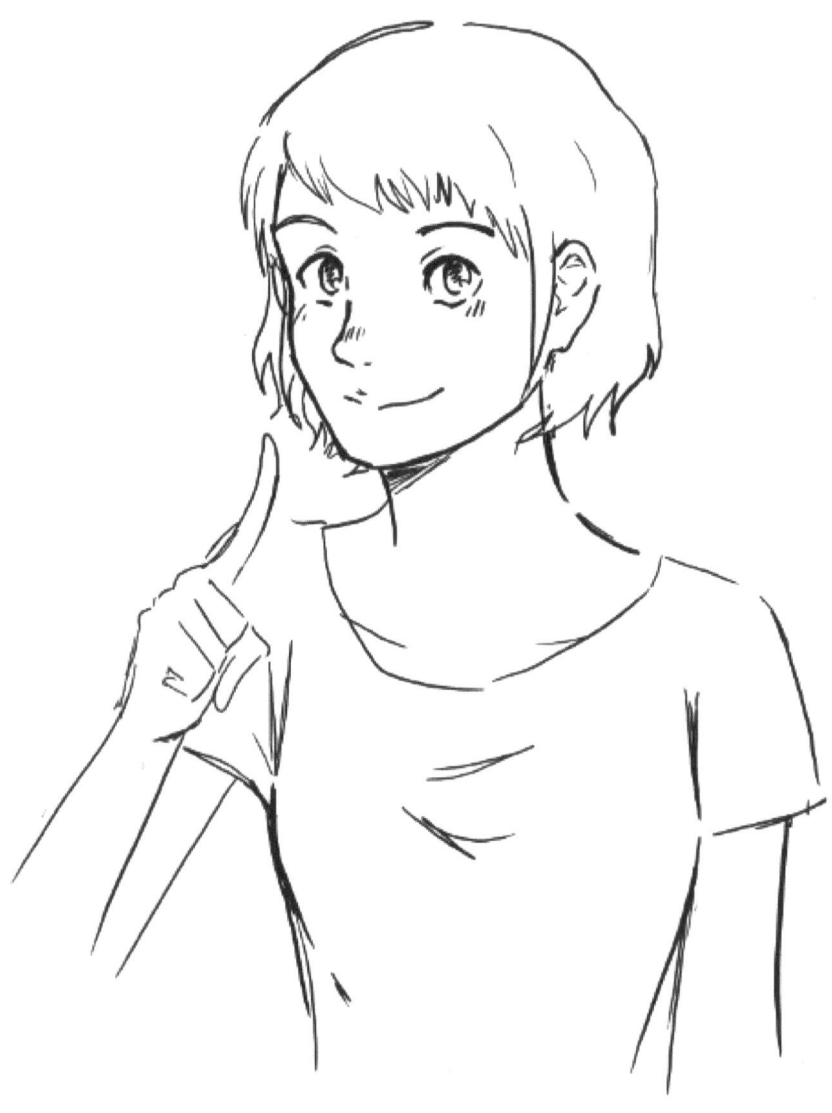

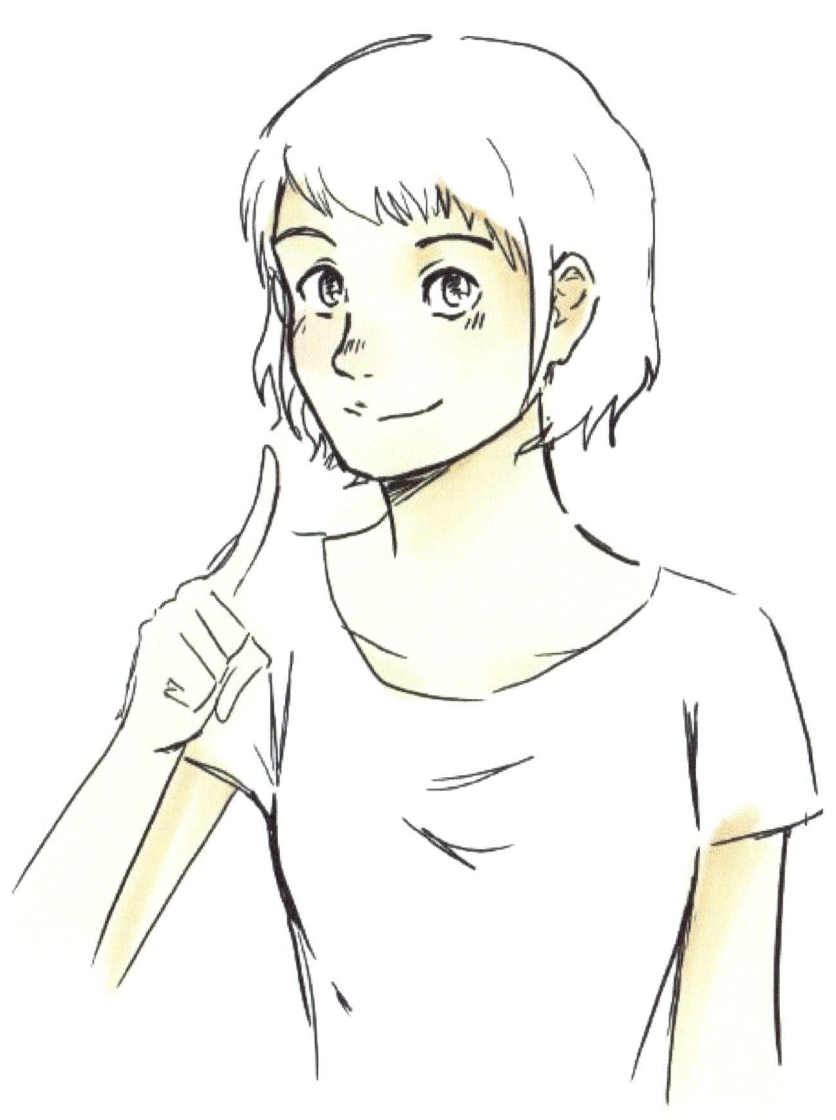

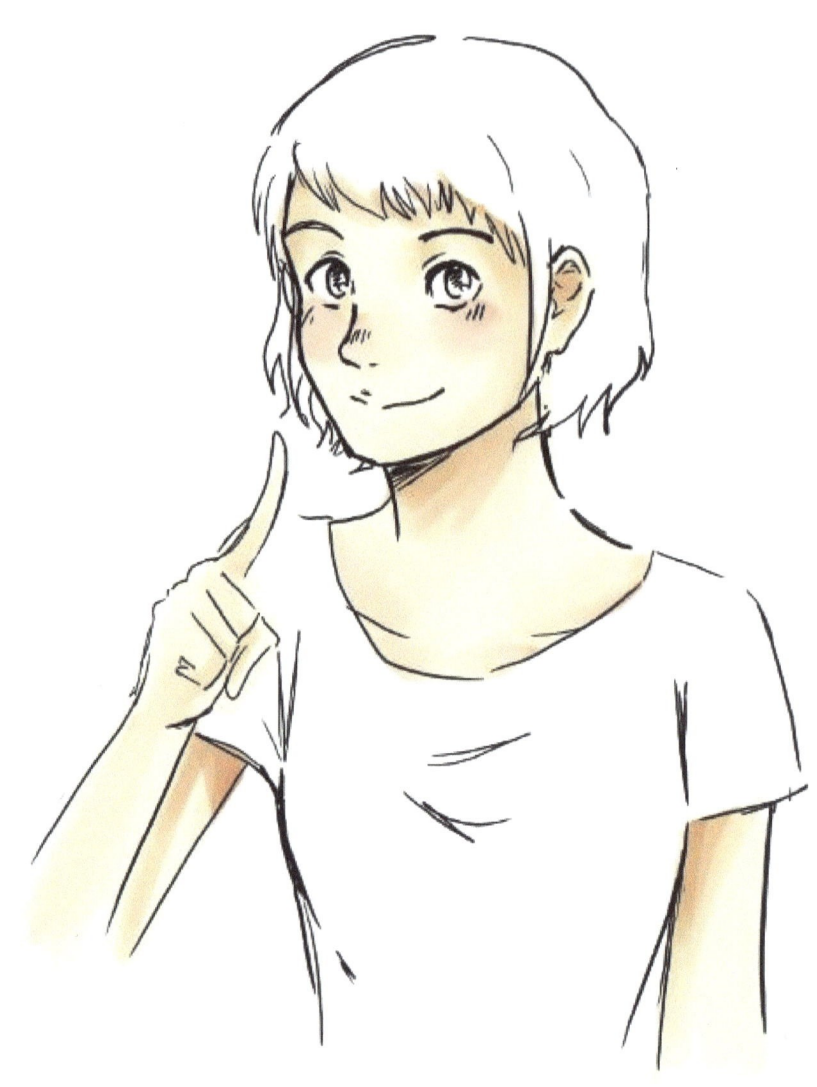

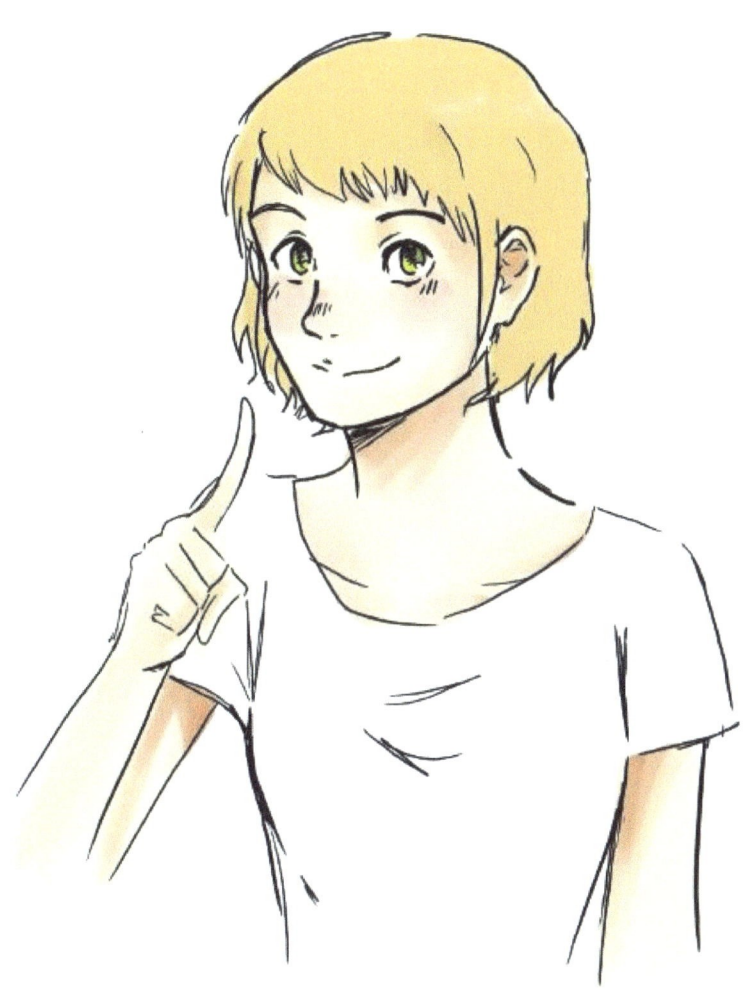

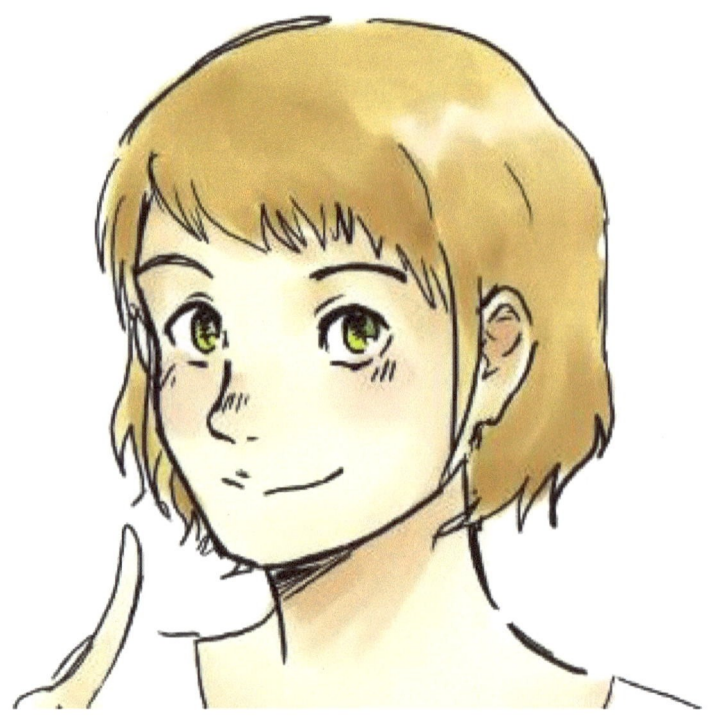

As for the hair, you can start with a light orange color then using a brown second tone, add more life to the hair by coloring the supposedly dark parts of the hair. Also, you can also see that there is a portion of the hair that wasn't' colored, This makes the hair glow.

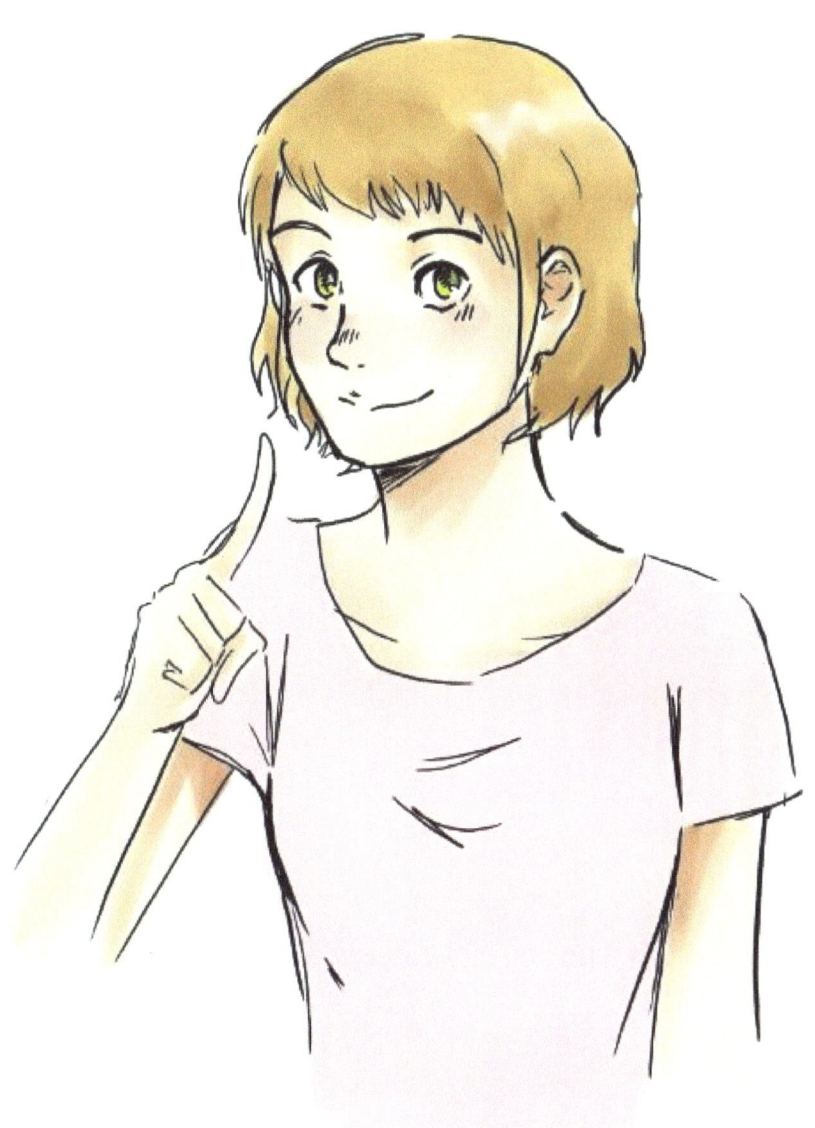

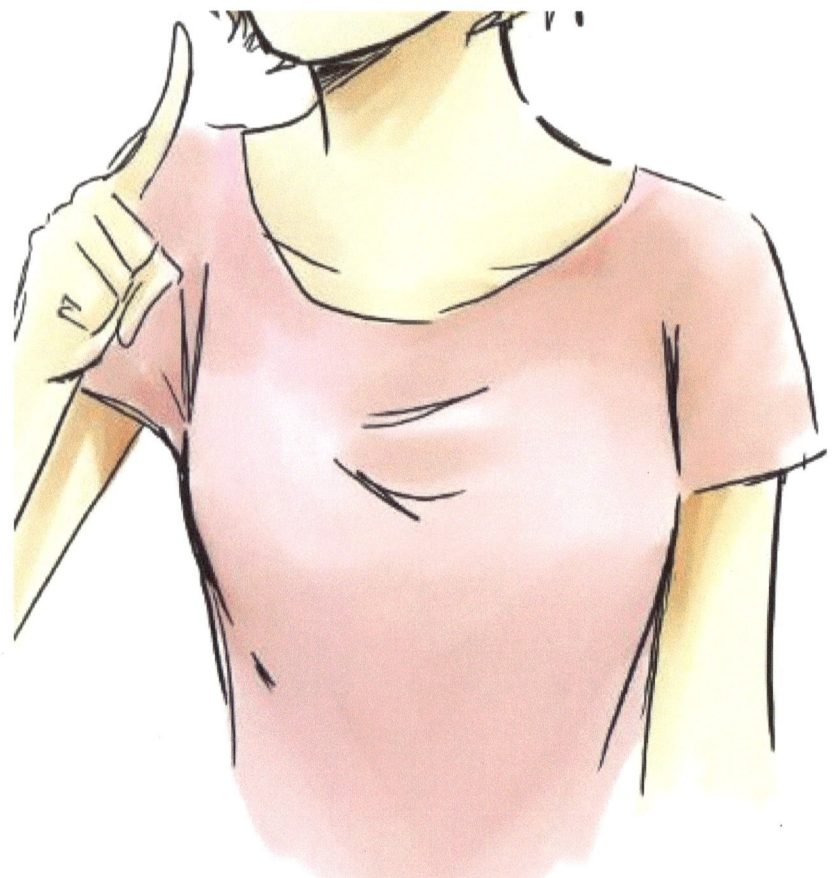

Clothes can be hard to color since you have to emphasize the shape of the body. Start with the base color. For this drawing, the base color is pink. You should take note that when coloring the body of a girl, you should color the breast area properly since when it is neglected, the shape won't be properly emphasized. Also take note of the creases, This will create more places to put dark tones on.

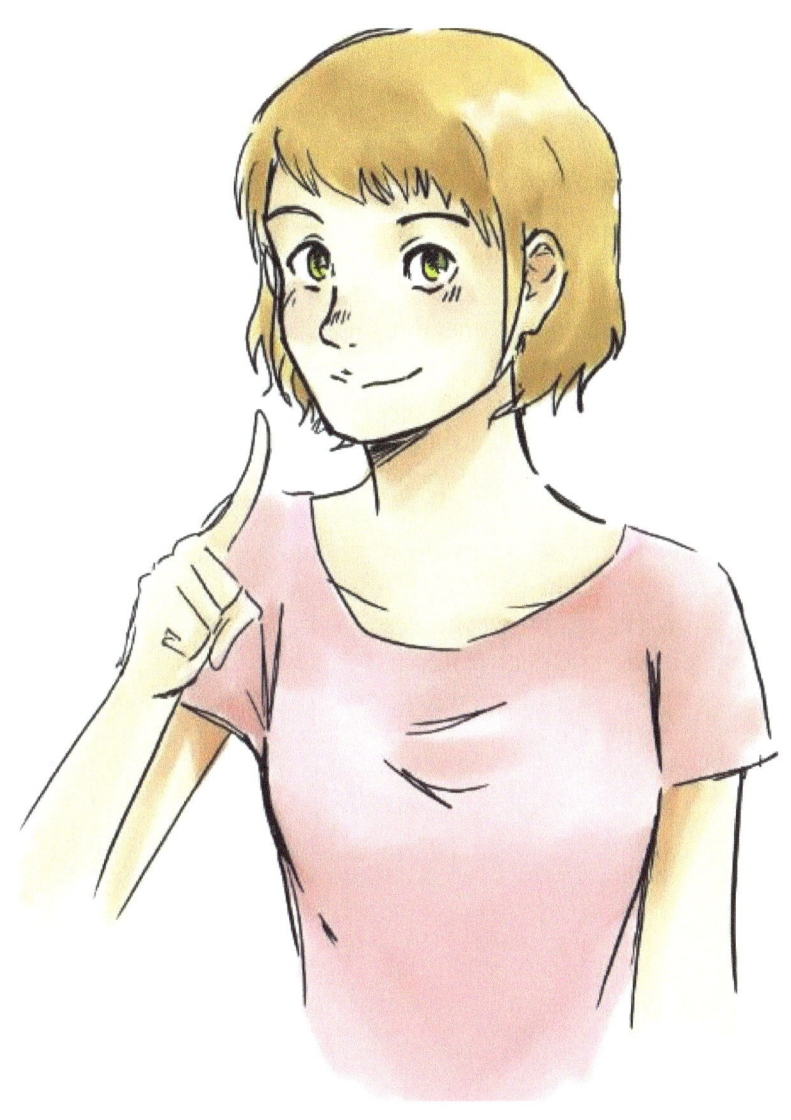

Done!!

Author Bio

Harriet Kim Anh B. Rodis

Being a young child, she has been inspired by the art of children story books her mother and father surrounded her with. From then on, she drew and drew---animals, plants, and things. She grew up in Indang, Cavite, Philippines where she also took up a course in BS Biology since she does not only took interest in drawing but also in Sciences. The place they had in Indang is rich in flora. They had gardens which yielded vegetables and flowers. To live in such a wonderful place inspired her to learn painting, too. You can see the young Harriet draw under the shade of the tree or next to their small and simple garden.

Due to financial problems, she was not able to take Fine Arts as course but she continued studying arts. She was known in the school as an artist good in drawing anime characters and making projects for Drafts. In college, she studied in Cavite State University and took up BS Biology where she excelled in Chemistry, Biology and Mathematics. She also applied in Gazette—the Official Student Publication unit of the university where she learned cartooning and using Photoshop. She also started working as an artist while studying.

In the year 2013, her family moved to Pampanga, Philippines; and so, she transferred to a different school, Angeles University Foundation, where she is currently continuing her studies in BS Biology.

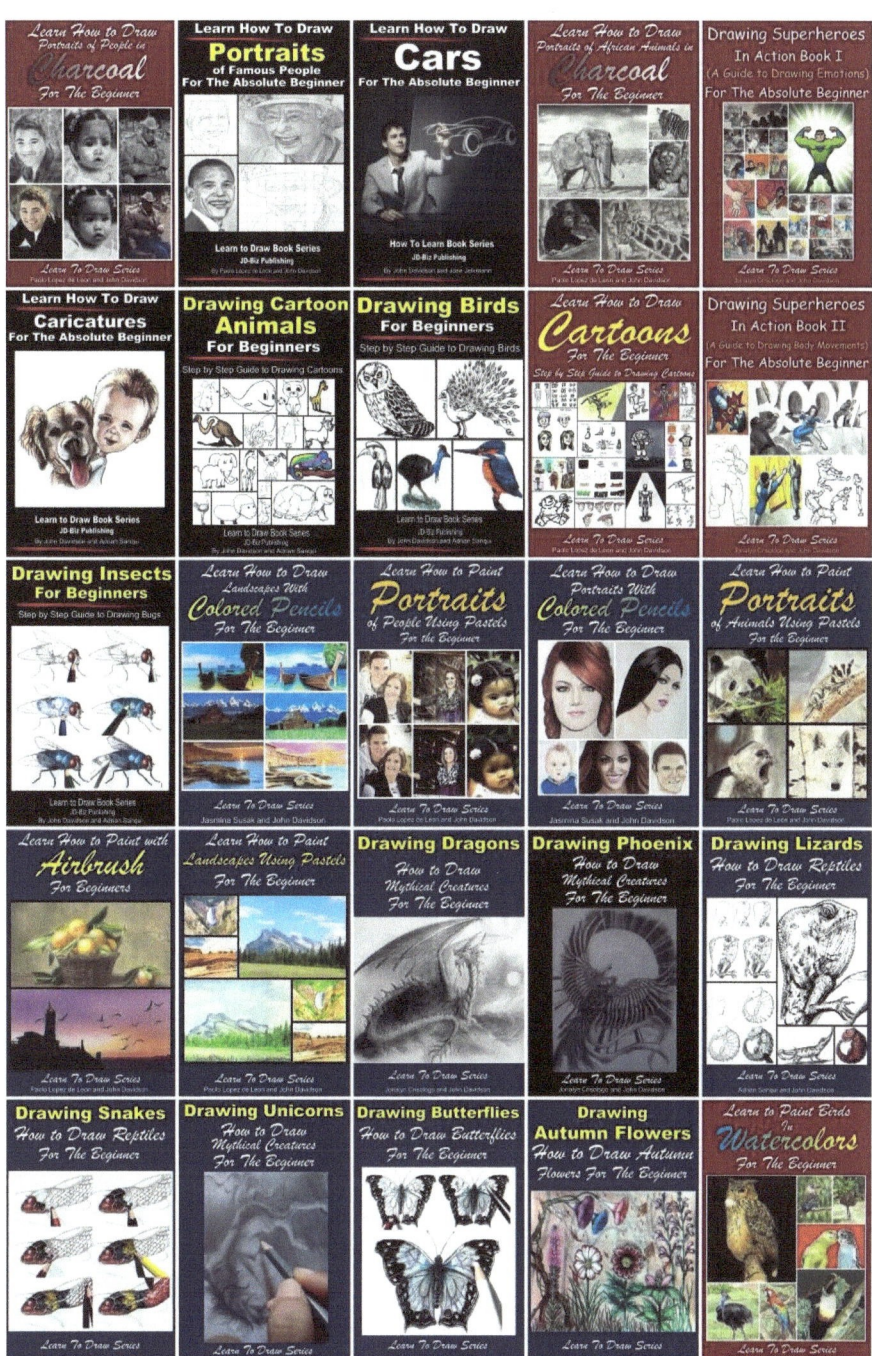

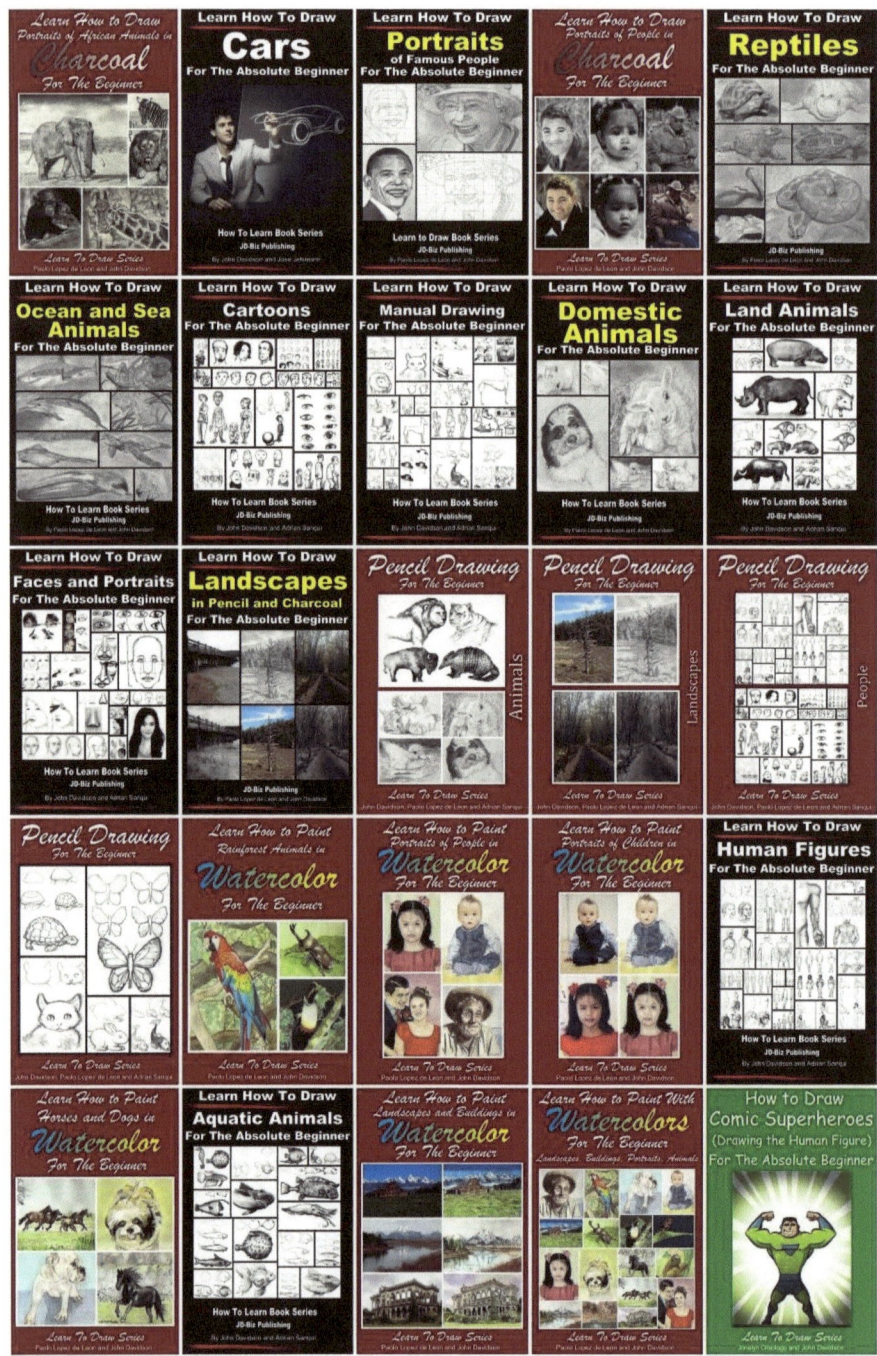

Publisher

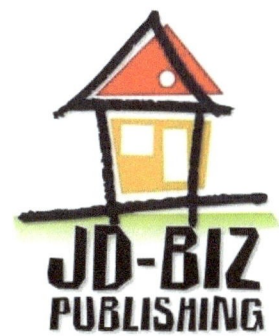

JD-Biz Corp

P O Box 374

Mendon, Utah 84325

http://www.jd-biz.com/

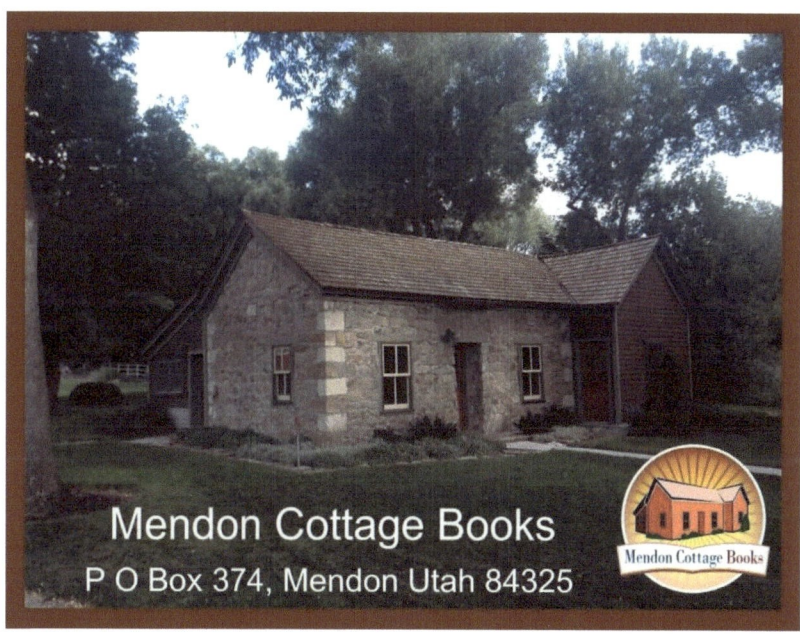

www.ingramcontent.com/pod-product-compliance
Lightning Source LLC
Chambersburg PA
CBHW040844180526
45159CB00001B/310